Y0-BCS-290

The Imitation of Christ

THOMAS À KEMPIS

THE IMITATION
OF CHRIST

TRANSLATED BY P. G. ZOMBERG

DUNSTAN PRESS

Copyright © 1984 by P. G. Zomberg

All rights reserved. No part of this book may be copied
or reproduced in any manner whatsoever without written
permission, except in the case of brief quotations
embodied in critical articles and reviews.

Nihil obstat:
    Rev. James E. Connor, C E N S O R   L I B R O R U M
Imprimatur:
    The Most Reverend Edward C. O'Leary, D. D.
    Bishop of Portland
    September 25, 1984

First edition.
Published in 1985
by Dunstan Press, 30 Linden Street, Rockland, Maine 04841

I S B N   0-930995-00-7

Library of Congress Catalog Card No. 84-71574

Printed in the United States of America

BV
4821
.Z66
1985

FOR JOAN,

WHO KNOWS WHY

Contents

NOTES ON THE ILLUSTRATIONS

Facing title page   "The Agony in the Garden." Wood engraving. Flemish school, *c.* 1430.

3   "Christ at the Pillory." Wood engraving. Flanders, *c.* 1450.

52   "Christ Bearing the Cross." Wood engraving. From John Mirk's *Festyuall* (Wynken de Worde, 1519).

84   "The Burial of Jesus." Wood engraving. From Thomas à Kempis's *Imytacyon of cryst* (Wynken de Worde, 1521?).

204   "The Last Supper." Wood engraving. English school, 15th century.

Translator's Introduction

This is, as C. S. Lewis once wrote, an astringent book. It is a challenging book, a tonic for pilgrim souls. It was meant to be so. But in its contents, it is not an "original" book. Its author, the Augustinian priest Thomas à Kempis (1380?–1471), was certainly capable of writing strong and often striking sentences. Many memorable passages show that he had a poet's gift for using words well. Nevertheless, the Imitation of Christ is on the whole an inspired gathering of the spiritual insights of many writers and contains more than a thousand allusions to passages in Sacred Scripture. Its special character as an unqualified call to spiritual perfection sets it apart from other spiritual writings in the Christian tradition. Next to the Bible, it has been perhaps the most influential book in the history of Christianity.

The Imitation of Christ is actually a collection of four separate works. The first is a summary of basic advice—or spiritual direction—addressed to a particular person who had chosen the life of a cloistered religious. The second is a discussion of what the interior or spiritual life entails, and concludes with the classic exposition of that life as following the "royal road of the Cross." The third book, its length equal to that of the first two books combined, discusses the consolations that attend a well-developed spiritual life. Many of the themes that the author had mentioned in the preceding works are here more fully developed, now in the form of a "conversation" between Christ and the soul of one who desires to become more like him. The fourth part of the Imitation is a meditation on the sacrament of the Eucharist.

Each part of the Imitation has a particular suitability for different persons at different times and on different occasions. Though originally written for men living (or preparing themselves to live) a formal religious life, its spiritual guidance is as applicable to women as to men. It was from the first appreciated as an ideal book of spiritual counsel for those on religious retreat. It is perfectly suited also for those times when a person feels keenly a need for spiritual renewal. The author intended that anyone with a sincere interest in becoming more like Christ be able to profit from his counsels. He took a realistic view of human nature and did not minimize the difficulties of reaching spiritual maturity. Nevertheless, one may say that his is the first book of the Christian tradition to be devoted mainly to showing the connection between fulfilling the requirements of faith and enjoying peace of mind in this life.

The original Latin text of the work is highly elliptical, but has none of the stilted (or "Latinate") quality of most existing English translations of it. Simple failures to appreciate the idioms of late-Latin prose mar most English translations of the work. The early English translations of the Imitation remain in print, couched in antique literary syntax and in words whose meanings have in many cases shifted to a measurable degree. Their artificial and usually excessive formality of tone would no doubt fail to win the approval of à Kempis. Scholars refer to the Latin style of the Imitation as "familiar" or "colloquial."

In the present translation, I have tried to convey the sense of the author's intention, as well as the sense of his words. I have consulted earlier translations as a check on the accuracy of my own; but because the idioms of late-Latin prose cannot be rendered adequately in a literal translation, I have provided a fuller wording of the author's thought whenever clarity was the result. I have indicated the source of direct quotations from Scripture, but not of paraphrases or indirect references. My goal has been to convey clearly the movement of the author's argument and open the riches of his book to the contemporary reader, in a style both plain and dignified.

As many readers of the Imitation of Christ are aware, its authorship has been questioned. To a large extent, debate on this subject has been a scholar's quarrel with no effect. Thomas à Kempis still has the best claim to be called the author. There is evidence that he composed each of the parts that make up the work. His contemporaries referred to him as the author; and one suspects that a sectarian interest, or a reluctance to admit that an "unknown" could have produced such a work, has been involved in attempts to prove them wrong.

In any case, it is of interest to know that Thomas à Kempis became the most important publicist for the renewal movement called Devotio Moderna. This "school" of spirituality took firm root in the Netherlands at the end of the fourteenth century. During the fifteenth century, it spread to Saxony, northern France, and Spain. Its founder was Gerald Groote (1340–84), whom some have preferred to call the author of the Imitation.

Thomas à Kempis was born in Kempen, Germany, near Cologne, and received his early schooling there and in Deventer, Holland. In Deventer, he came under the influence of the Brothers of the Common Life, promoters of religious devotion inspired by the example of the first Christians. While a student, he became a skilled scribe and produced many fine manuscripts for the community at Deventer. After completing his studies there, he joined in the founding of a new Augustinian monastic community at Mount St. Agnes near Zwolle; and in 1413 he was ordained priest. He wrote numerous works, including a history of the Mount St. Agnes monastery. A motto attributed to him is: I have sought rest everywhere and found it nowhere, except in little nooks with little books. The work for which he is best known, the Imitation of Christ, was first collected in manuscript form in 1418. Manuscripts of each of the four "books" exist dated 1427. A copy written by à Kempis himself in 1441 survives, and has been published in facsimile (Brussels, 1956). The work was one of the first to be published in printed form (1473) and has been numerous times translated into the major languages.

Followers of the Devotio Moderna—who were reacting against the growing laxity of the Church's governing hierarchy—promoted a spirituality based on the example of Jesus, on devotion to the Passion and the Eucharist, on a formal plan of meditation, on self-mortification, on insistence that divine and human goods be rightly ordered, on withdrawal from attachment to material things, on devotional reading of Scripture, and on a skeptical attitude toward the value of scholarship or human culture.

One might question whether the Imitation of Christ, reflecting as it does that same mix of spiritual values, continues to have relevance in our day. Certainly many contemporary spiritual writers have recommended it as still "the richest spiritual fare" (Frank Sheed). C. S. Lewis, Bishop Fulton J. Sheen, and many others have drawn from it in their own writings and often commended it to others. It had a very important influence on the spirituality of many saints, notably Sir Thomas More and Thérèse of Lisieux.

The reason for the work's perennial popularity is that it speaks simply, clearly, and often eloquently about the heart of Christian faith and spirituality. It is evident that since the time when the Imitation of Christ was first written, human life has become so tightly wrapped up in material goods that spiritual values are quickly suffocated in individual human lives. Then too, religious fashions come and go, but the need to protect oneself from current fashions does not change. The Imitation of Christ is excellent food for people starving for spiritual sustenance; and it helps them sort out what is passing from what is abiding. As Thomas Merton wrote, "contemplation, asceticism, mental prayer, and unworldliness are elements that most need to be rediscovered by Christians of our time" (The Ascent to Truth, 1951). The Imitation of Christ promotes those very ideals. Like Piers Plowman, another "reform tract" written at the end of the fourteenth century, it calls the followers of Christ "to live a lowly life in the lore of Holy Church."

The Imitation of Christ has appealed to people in all walks of life. Part of its appeal is the thoroughness with which it "opens" the spirituality of the New Testament to anyone desiring to advance in the Christian virtues. One draws from it a key insight: the ability to see one's life against the background of eternity, and to understand that a loving God entered human history and changed the idea of history. But perhaps the most attractive quality of the Imitation of Christ is its uncompromising insistence that no one can serve two masters (I. xvii). In countless ways, it calls us back to the spirituality of the New Testament and, indeed, forces us to pay close attention to it.

P. G. Z.

The Imitation of Christ

Book One

The Imitation of Christ

Counsels for the Spiritual Life

i. *To imitate Christ is to despise this world's vanities.*
THE LORD says, "Whoever follows me does not walk in darkness." These words of Christ tell us that if we imitate him in his life and in his habits, we will be truly enlightened and the blindness of our hearts will be cured. Let us then decide to study carefully the life of Christ.

The teachings of Christ are superior to all the teachings of the saints. In his teachings we find, as it were, a hidden manna. Yet it sometimes happens that because we hear the gospel so frequently, we lose our taste for it; and thus we lose also the spirit of Christ's teachings. So if we are to hear the words of Christ with new ears, we need to try to make his life a model for our lives.

If you are one of those who can talk learnedly about the Holy Trinity, but lack the virtue of humility, how have you done yourself any service by displeasing the Trinity? As you know, it is not your skill at talking that makes you holy or just; only the virtues of your life endear you to God. It is far better to *be* repentant than to know what repentance is in so many words. Even if you knew the entire Bible by heart, and also the teachings of all the philosophers, what good would that do you if you lacked the love and grace of God?

Yes, vanity of vanities: all is vanity except one thing, and that is loving God and serving him alone. That is the best wisdom—to strive first for the heavenly kingdom, rather than for any earthly prize.

To seek after riches, to base one's whole life on that goal, is surely vain. To seek worldly honors, to wish to be held in high esteem, to pamper the desires of the flesh, to covet what we have no right to, to become overly concerned about how long we shall live, to give little thought to the moral character of our lives—all these are rightly called vanities.

To be exclusively concerned about the things of this life on earth, and to neglect the future life that God has prepared for us—that too is vanity. It is vanity to devote one's life to passing pleasures rather than to the promise of everlasting joy.

There is a true proverb that applies here: *The eye is not satisfied to see, nor the ear to hear.* We may take this to mean that we are wise to fix our hearts' affections on invisible goods, rather than limit our love to visible *things.* The alternative is to become blind to our own consciences and lose God's grace.

ii. *How to cultivate the virtue of true humility.*

Each of us has a natural curiosity about the world we live in. But we need to ask ourselves what our knowledge is worth if we do not know our true relationship to the Creator. It is clear that the lowly peasant who lives as a child of God is more to be admired than the learned astronomer who can plot the movements of the stars but who completely neglects his spiritual life.

If a man knows himself well and truly, he sees and admits his weaknesses and faults; and he does not glory in any praise that others may give him. So I must consider, for example, that if I am very learned but not charitable, my knowledge will be of precious little use to me when I come to stand before the God who will judge my life.

It is possible to desire to know too much; in that desire lie many idle distractions and much foolishness. Some persons are learned and enjoy displaying their knowledge so that they will be thought wise. There are many things we each *could* know, but would bring us no spiritual benefit. It is simply not wisdom to be distracted by anything that does not assist our spiritual progress.

The display of our knowledge does not satisfy our souls. Rather, it is the goodness of our lives that brings a comfort to our minds. An upright conscience enables us to place our trust in God.

We may even go so far as to say that the more knowledge we possess, and the more surely we possess it, the more surely that knowledge will be questioned on the Day of Judgment unless our lives are also holy. We have no reason to puff ourselves up because of any of our talents; rather, we need to concern ourselves about the use we make of them.

No matter how much you or I have come to know, we can be sure that there are a great many more things about which we are wholly ignorant. When we are tempted to think highly of ourselves, we should remember not only how ignorant we are, but that many others are more learned, more expert, than we. The one thing we do need to learn is to prefer to be unknown and unappreciated.

That is a very difficult, but a spiritually profitable, lesson. Not to think highly of oneself, always to think highly of others, is not only wise counsel, but a way to spiritual perfection. If you should see someone commit a fault or even a crime, do not use that as an occasion to think you are a better person; for how long will it be before you lapse into unholiness? Each of us is spiritually weak; we have no reason to think that we are less weak than others.

iii. *What we can learn from Truth itself.*

Lucky is that person who has been taught not by words and signs but by studying Truth as it is in itself. Our opinions about the truth of things are often mistaken; for our senses help us see the truth only partially and imperfectly. And yet so often we find ourselves arguing about matters concerning which we know little or nothing. On the Day of Judgment, our ignorance about esoteric things is not what will be held against us.

Having "eyes that do not see," we tend to interest ourselves in this or that out of curiosity and sometimes actually harm ourselves as a result; while at the same time neglecting other aspects of our lives that we should attend to for our own good.

The person who listens to the eternal Word is not likely to pose as an opinion-maker. From that one Word, all created things have their existence; and only through that Word do all things "speak." Apart from that Word—that Beginning of true speaking—none of us can understand or judge anything rightly. On the other hand, if we can learn to see all creation in relation to that One, our hearts will be able to know the peace that comes to those who place their trust in him.

> O God of Truth,
> > may my love for you last forever.
> The knowledge that comes to me
> > through seeing and hearing
> seldom satisfies my desire to know the Truth;
> > only you can satisfy that desire.
> All human creatures, all earthly creatures,
> > stand silent before your Truth,
> > so that you alone can speak to me.

If a person is free from internal contradictions and conflicts, the more easily does he or she understand the truth of things; for such a person is enlightened by heavenly Truth. The person who keeps from becoming enmeshed in numerous kinds of busy-ness remains free to serve the honor of God with a steadfast spirit and with simplicity of heart. The best way for us to find internal peace of mind is by freeing ourselves from all forms of *self*-seeking.

The good person thinks carefully before following any inclinations of the heart. In that way, evil inclinations are put to the test of a well-formed judgment.

The hardest obstacle any of us has to overcome is our self. So your main effort should be to take charge of your inclinations. Your goal is to become each day a better master of your life.

In this life, just as we never see anything with total clarity, so too we find some imperfection in even the best works of human skill. The way to find God is not through advanced studies, but through humility of heart and through a sure knowledge of our own weaknesses.

There is nothing wrong with knowledge as such, nor can anyone be blamed for wishing to learn about a subject. Knowledge is a good thing; God made us for knowing. But compared to knowledge, a good conscience and a virtuous life are far better and more admirable. History shows us many examples of persons who loved and sought after knowledge but neglected their spiritual lives; they not only fell into evil ways but have left us little if anything of value as a fruit of their learning.

Would that more people worked as hard at weeding out vices and planting virtues in themselves as they do at fueling heated arguments about what is or is not true in human knowledge. All this one-sided interest has resulted in scandalous moral evil in people's lives and laxity among the clergy. On the Day of Judgment, we, like they, will not be asked what tomes we have read or how well we have spoken, but what we have done and how devoutly we have lived.

Think of all those once-famous scholars and experts: even their immediate successors do not remember them. Their fame was not worth remembering.

And that reminds us that the glory of the world passes quickly. If a person's life is equal in excellence to his or her learning, at least that person has studied well and with good effects. On the other hand, those who search for worldly glory have no true greatness in them, and their ambition dooms them to be soon forgotten. Truly great are the charitable, kindly persons who do not boast of their accomplishments. It is spiritual wisdom to seek the highest prize—Christ—and to look upon earthly goods as of little value by comparison. To be truly learned is to seek always to do God's will and to put one's own will in second place.

iv. *Judge others with prudence.*
As a rule, we should be cautious about accepting whatever another person says or recommends to us. In each case, weigh what is told you by considering what God's will may be. We need to be on guard especially against being quick to accept malicious gossip; for we are more likely to believe something evil than something good about another person. Human nature is weak and prone to evil, and talebearers are prone to exaggerate—so a prudent person avoids listening to idle reports about the faults of others.

Similarly, if we would be wise, we will not jump to any conclusions or make any rash decisions about what we ought to do. Nor will we be obstinate in promoting our own opinions. And just as we should not lend our ears to gossip, so too should we refrain from passing it on to others.

It is often the wisest course to get advice from a conscientious person and to follow it rather than one's own inclinations. A holy person shares in God's own wisdom and has more useful "experience" to draw on—and to share with others. The more humble a person is, the more inclined toward God, the more prudent in decision-making, and the more at peace.

v. *How to read the Holy Scriptures.*

When you read from Sacred Scripture, seek for religious truth, not literary elegance. In that way, you will be reading it in the same spirit in which it was written. One should approach Scripture as a source of spiritual profit, not as a collection of scientific documents. So too, one ought to read both the simpler and the more profound books of the Bible, without letting the "authority" of the various authors sway one's interests. Let your love of God's truth lead you to read every part of Scripture.

As you read, pay more attention to *what is said* than to *who is saying it.* The human authors of Scripture have all passed away; but the truth of God remains available to us through their words. As you know, God speaks to us in many ways, through all kinds of persons.

You may find that your own curiosity gets in the way of your profiting from reading Scripture, because you find yourself stopping over various passages, seeking to know more or to enter into debate, when you should simply read farther. To profit from Scripture, you should read with humility, sincerity, and faith, and, of course, *not* so as to become regarded as an expert.

Do not hesitate to read also the writings of the saints; and listen attentively to those who have a responsibility for your spiritual welfare—for what they say to you is not said without a good reason.

vi. *How to deal with your appetites and passions.*

The person who desires anything (except God) *too much* is not at peace. The proud or envious person is never satisfied. Only those who live humbly and simply are entirely at peace in their souls.

Persons who have not mastered themselves soon "give in" to themselves in small things. Those who are spiritually weak and who have not won control of the body's appetites are not able to free themselves from slavery to earthly things. If they do succeed in denying themselves some earthly good, they are then unhappy and tend to react crossly to anyone who annoys them. Yet if they give in to their appetites, they find that their conscience will not let them be happy—and they are none the closer to the peace and contentment they are seeking.

They have not yet discovered that it is by resisting passions and regulating appetites that one becomes no longer a slave to them and finds peace of heart. The earth-bound person, whose life is one of searching for new amusements and distractions, does not have that peace. The devout person alone has it.

vii.   *Place your hope chiefly in God.*

It hardly needs saying that anyone who puts trust in other people or in created things is likely to know disappointment. There is no shame, of course, in our serving others for the love of Jesus Christ, or in adopting a life of poverty. Those who do such things place their hope in God, not in themselves. If each of us does the good that it is in our power to perform, God will use us as his instruments. God helps the humble, and humbles those who think they don't need God.

If you are wealthy, if you have influential friends, give glory and thanks to God, the giver of all our benefits. Remember that the most important thing God desires to give us is himself. Do not take undue pride in the strength or beauty of your body—both fade away at the slightest sickness. The talents and aptitudes you received from your parents become displeasing to God if you act as if he was not really the source of those benefits too.

Do not be quick to regard yourself as superior to other persons, for it may be that, in God's eyes, you are *less* worthy than they. Only God knows every person truly. In the same way, don't be too quick to praise your own deeds. God will judge them in his own way. Certainly some things that many people like to praise are actually displeasing to God.

No matter what your own virtues are, always be ready to think others more virtuous; in that way you can retain a proper humility. It will do you no harm to consider yourself the least of God's human creatures; but you will do yourself immense harm if you assume and behave as if, in his eyes, you are superior to any other person. The heart of the proud man is set in turmoil by envy, and frequently also by anger. Apart from humility there can be no peace of heart.

viii. *Be discreet in sharing confidences.*

Do not reveal the secrets of your heart to every acquaintance, especially to those who are young and inexperienced. Instead, seek the counsel and the guidance of someone who is wise and spiritually close to God. Do not imitate those who think they can get ahead by flattering the rich or associating with influential people. Prefer instead the company of sensible, self-disciplined, and devout persons, whose conversations are free of self-promotion.

Our attitude toward others ought to be one of charitable concern. It is a mistake to think that every person you meet can be your close friend. It sometimes happens that people do not live up to the good reputation attributed to them. It may happen that your attempts to force your company on others will only let them know your own weaknesses.

Seek first, therefore, a close friendship with God and the angels, and then with those who will assist that friendship.

ix. *Submit to the authority of religious superiors.*

There is much to be said for those who live in faithful obedience to their religious superiors. It is true that we all prefer to act as we choose, just as we are inclined to like those whose tastes and preferences are the same as ours. Yet we have to admit that there is a sense of security that comes with obedience to our religious superiors. Is it not often said that it is easier and safer to accept a command than to give it?

Many seem to accept religious obedience because they have no choice, rather than because they love God. They are the ones who take exception at every opportunity to their superiors' decisions. For such persons, there can be no peace of heart until they accept the authority of their superiors as God's will for them. Some of them have tried to solve this "problem" by moving to another religious house or order—and have been deceived.

If we can trust that God is with us, we have enough reason to set aside our own preferences for the sake of peace in the community. Because none of us can always know what is best, we should be willing to set our own opinions aside so that the preferences of others can be considered. Even if you are convinced that what you prefer would be for the best, you will be better off to support the opinion of your religious superior *if* you do so as God's will for you.

x. *Avoid idle chatter.*

Try to keep yourself away from the hubbub of current events; your interest in the affairs of the world may be well intentioned but can easily become a preoccupation. The vanity of desiring to be a participant in mighty affairs easily takes hold in us, and betrays us. I have often wished, after I had gotten involved in some idle talk, that I had kept silent.

Why should we be so ready for gab and gossip when afterward, in a moment of silent reflection, our conscience chides us for it? One reason, of course, is that we enjoy conversing with others; it is a source of consolation or comfort and eases the pains of our hearts. Another reason is that we enjoy stating our likes and dislikes, and we think that they entitle us to spend time arguing with others about them. But how often is our conversation merely a sign of our vainness, rather than being of any purpose? The little satisfactions we get from conversation of that sort actually tend to keep us away from spiritual growth and divine consolations.

Let us be on our guard and pray for the grace to avoid wasteful chattering. If we guard our speech, so that it consists of appropriate comments, we are unlikely to get caught up in bad habits that hinder our spiritual development. On the other hand, to speak with others with sincerity about spiritual things can assist our spiritual progress, especially when those with whom we speak share our interest in the growth of our spiritual life, as children of God.

xi. *Set selfish habits aside.*

Think how peaceful our lives would be if we were not so busy hanging on the latest sayings and doings of others, or getting involved in things that do not properly concern us.

Those who get themselves entangled in other people's desires, or who are constantly looking to please themselves, or who never stop for moments of recollection—how can they be at peace? Blessed are the single-hearted: *they* shall have peace.

Recall that some of the saints reached a stage of perfection and a skill at contemplation by setting aside all their earthly desires. Their self-mortification allowed them to cling to God and to focus their thoughts on him. We, on the other hand, are so concerned to feed our own appetites and so anxious about temporary problems that we don't leave ourselves any time for self-reform. Failing to eliminate even one fault in ourselves, we go on in our cold or lukewarm fashion.

Unless we can keep our hearts from turmoil and become, as it were, dead to ourselves, we will be unable to appreciate the things of God or experience a taste of heavenly contemplation.

In this battle against ourselves, we must be valiant soldiers, trusting that the Lord stands ready to help us with his grace. He alone is the source of our spiritual weapons in this struggle for self-mastery.

Some people make the mistake of thinking that their progress in religion can be measured by their participation in outward observances. The peace of mind that comes from true religion, however, is something that we shall not experience until we lay ax to the root of our selfishness—our passions.

If each of us were to cut away the root of one vice every year, we would soon become perfect. Yet it happens more often that a person is more holy in the period following first conversion than after many years as a believer. Instead of growing in faith and devoutness, a person is thought to do well to retain at least some of that original fervor.

If we would only be more demanding of ourselves at the start, we would find it easy to carry out our daily duties with ease and joy.

Our old habits do not die easily; and our will is even harder to oppose. But unless we begin to overcome our lesser appetites, how can we expect to overcome the stronger ones? It is much easier to resist temptations at the start and avoid falling into an evil habit. Once the habit is ours, it is likely to lead us on to worse things. If we could only see what peace of mind comes with a holy life, and what joy such a life brings to others, we would be much more anxious to make spiritual progress.

xii. *Adversity has value for us.*
Sometimes, it is good for us to experience troubles and difficulties. They can teach us a truth about ourselves: that this life is actually a time of exile, and that we cannot place our hopes in this world. In the same way, if others sometimes oppose us or think ill of us, even when our behavior and intentions have been above re-

proach, we can accept it as a sign that we need to prefer humility to pride. At such times, we are moved to recall that what God thinks of us is what matters, and that if we have the consolations of God, we will be less inclined to seek the approval of our fellow men.

When a good person experiences some trouble or temptation—such as evil thoughts—he understands well that God is his best protector. Grieved by his sufferings, he prays and speaks to God about them. He may speak of his weariness and even pray for the blessing of death, so that he may be united with Christ. At such a moment, he well understands that perfect security and peace cannot be found in this life.

xiii. *Be ready to resist temptation.*

So long as we live in this world, we cannot avoid temptation or suffering. When one temptation or adversity passes, another takes its place. We shall always know suffering in some form or other. In the Book of Job, we read: "The life of man upon earth is a warfare" (7.1). Indeed it is. And therefore each person must pray and watch, lest the devil, who sleeps not but prowls the earth in search of someone to devour, find a way to deceive him. None of us is so holy or perfect that we are never tempted. Our human nature is subject to temptation, because we have lost the state of blessedness in which God made man.

Yet temptations, though often troubling, can be useful to us; they can humble, purify, and instruct us. Have not the saints been tempted often and severely, and have they not profited from successfully resisting temptations? Certainly many others who did not resist became like animals and lost something of their humanity.

If all we do is "resist" temptations and make no effort to cut out the root of selfishness, we will not only fail to make any spiritual progress but will find ourselves falling behind. It is only with patience, humility, and the help of God that we can overcome temptations. Your own unaided efforts, no matter how harsh a penance you impose on yourself, will not be effective. When you are tempted, seek the advice of your spiritual director; and when you see others tempted, be ready to counsel them as you would wish to be counseled.

All temptation to evil begins in imperfect faith and a wavering trust in God. Those whose faith wavers, whose resolve is weak, are most subject to temptation. They are like ships without rudders, at the mercy of the waves. A just man, on the other hand, is actually steeled by temptation—as fire tempers iron. We often are ignorant about what progress we have made; the way we deal with temptations reveals to us the sort of persons we are.

It has been well said: "Resist the beginnings; remedies come too late when, by long delay, the evil has gained strength." The Enemy is more easily resisted when first encountered outside the door of the mind and kept from crossing the threshold. Once allowed into the mind, Satan captures the imagination, wakens the passions, and little by little breaks down the resistance of the will. Hence, the more slowly a temptation is resisted, the weaker we become in coping with the next one, and the more power the Enemy has over us.

Different persons experience a different pattern of temptation; some are sorely tempted shortly after their conversion, others toward the end of their lives, and still others more or less constantly. Some are but mildly tempted—such is the providence of God, who knows the character of every person and desires the salvation of all. We must therefore never despair when we are tempted, but pray more fervently that God will assist us. As Saint Paul wrote: "You can trust God not to allow you to be tried beyond your strength, and with every trial he will give you a way out of it" (1 Corinthians 10.13). Let us therefore place our souls under God's protection; he will save and exalt the humble in spirit. Look upon your temptations as a way to measure your merit and virtue in God's eyes.

It is not at all surprising that a person should be devout when he experiences no trials or tribulations; but if he bears his difficulties with much patience, then one may hold high hopes for his spiritual progress. Some persons seem never to experience a temptation to serious evil, yet are frequently overcome by temptations in small things; such persons should mark well, and be humbled by the thought, that they must never presume to be able to resist the stronger temptation when it comes.

xiv. *Be slow to judge others.*

Examine your conscience and take care to avoid passing judgment on the behavior of others. Passing judgment on others is a sign of vanity, is often erroneous in its results, and may even be sinful. How common it is that we judge ourselves to be better than we are!

We are too likely to think that we ourselves are as we wish to be; in the thicket of our feelings, we lose perspective. If we really cared only for God's opinion of us, we would not become so upset whenever others oppose us in our opinions. As it is, we are very likely to get swept up by some interior or external force and conform our opinions to it. There are many who, without knowing it, act always out of self-interest. When events unfold in ways they approve of, they think themselves happy; when events unfold otherwise, the same persons feel frustrated and unhappy.

All too often, differences of opinion or judgment lead to dissension and bitterness, even among friends and relatives, even among devout or religious persons. How difficult it is to give up an old habit; and how reluctant we are to be led farther than our own vision extends.

Certainly, if we rely more on our wit or efforts than on accepting the governance of Jesus Christ, we will only rarely—and then only very slowly— become enlightened persons. What God wishes is that we submit to his will completely and, by living with his love, surpass the limitations of human wisdom.

xv. *Let charity be the motive of your actions.*

Everything you do should be done not for any worldly motive or out of human respect, but out of consideration for the needs of another. In the latter case, you *may* put off rendering another a favor today for the sake of doing him a better one tomorrow.

Unless charity is your motive, your external works are of no spiritual profit to you; on the other hand, even the smallest act of kindness done out of concern for the welfare of another is very fruitful. God is more interested in, and counts as of greater value, the motive of love than the number of good works that spring from it. He who loves much, does much. He who does a thing well also does much. Doing a thing well means doing it for the sake of the common good, rather than out of self-interest.

But do not be deceived: what looks like charity is often an act of selfishness. The motives by which people commonly act are these: bodily appetites, a hope for reward, a preference for ease and comfort, and plain self-interest. The truly charitable person, however, seeks to glorify God rather than please himself. Not desiring praise for himself, he envies no one. Desiring to glorify God, he praises God for all human goods, as their source. He sees God as a fountain, in whose waters all the blessed will one day experience peace and joy forever. Any persons who have a spark of true charity in their hearts can see that all merely earthly things are vanities, vanities.

xvi. *Deal patiently with the faults of others.*

Until God changes the conditions of our existence, we should deal patiently with the faults we cannot mend —in ourselves as well as in others. Perhaps God allows such faults in order to test us; for until we develop patience in the face of trials, our merits will be of little value. Certainly we should pray that God will help us bear up with annoyances, by teaching us the spirit of patient acceptance.

If a person has had a fault reprimanded but fails to amend it, do not nag him about it; instead, commend him to God, and pray that God's will may be reflected in the lives of all his servants. God best knows how to bring good out of evil.

So be patient with whatever defects and infirmities you find in others. Keep in mind that you yourself are in some ways a burden to others. If you have difficulty being the person you think you should be, how much more difficult it would be to try to make another person more to your liking.

How ready we are to wish other persons were perfect! Would that we worked as hard at eliminating our own defects. We much prefer to see others corrected than to accept any correction of our own behavior. We begrudge others the freedom they enjoy, yet fight against having our own freedom or privileges restricted. We think that others should conform their lives to rules and regulations, while we do as we please.

If it were the case that all people were perfect, how could we suffer for the sake of God? It is God's will that we learn to bear one another's burdens. No one is without some defect; everyone carries some burden; no one is completely self-sufficient or sufficiently wise. We need to support one another, offering comfort, assistance, and instruction; and we need to admonish one another, too. A person's true value becomes clear when a time of trouble comes; for adversity does not weaken us, but shows what sort of persons we are.

xvii. *Those who choose to live in religious communities must learn self-discipline.*

If you would live at peace in a religious community, you must discipline your will in many ways. It is not a simple matter to live day in, day out, in such a community without complaint, and to persevere in such a life till one's death. Those religious who succeed in living a holy life and end their days on earth in a happy death are truly blessed.

The key to persevering in your search for spiritual perfection is thinking of yourself as a pilgrim in exile on earth. If you desire to become a truly "religious" person, accept your role as a fool for the sake of Christ. Donning a religious garment and having the hair tonsured work little change in a person; the truly religious person is one who has radically changed his life and subdued his appetites.

If you have for yourself any goals other than God and the salvation of your soul, you will find only trouble and sorrow in religious life. Furthermore, if it is not your goal to become the lowest servant of all, you cannot know much peace of mind. After all, you entered religious life in order to serve, not to rule; to labor and suffer, not to lie about in idle conversation. In religious community life, among one's fellows, one is tried, like gold in a furnace. No one can prosper in such a life unless his chief desire is to place himself humbly in God's service.

xviii. *Learn from the example of our holy predecessors.*
Consider the clear example set for us by the saints; from them shines the light of true perfection and religion. Consider how little we do by comparison—and how poorly our lives, alas, compare to theirs. The saints—those close friends of Christ—served him in hunger and thirst, cold and nakedness, exhausting labors, vigils and fasts, prayers and holy meditations, despite persecutions and numberless obstacles. They willingly suffered many trials, because they set themselves to follow the footsteps of Christ. All of them— Apostles, martyrs, confessors, virgins, and many more —put a higher value on the prospect of eternal life than on their earthly lives.

Consider also how strictly the holy hermits lived in the desert; yet they suffered terrible temptations, being frequently attacked by the Enemy. They observed rigorous fasts and were driven by a zeal for spiritual perfection. They fought bravely against their evil habits, and kept their focus on God. During the day, they labored; in the night, they prayed for long hours at a time. Even during their labors, their minds were turned to God in meditation. They knew how to use their time well; and every hour they gave to God passed quickly. Through the gift of contemplation, they were able to live without concern for bodily refreshment. They put behind them all concern for riches, dignities, honors, friends, and relatives; desiring none of this world's goods, they did not concern themselves about supplying the needs of the body—in fact, they found those needs a bother. Poor in earthly things, they were rich in grace and virtue, and in divine consolation. Strangers to the world, they were close friends of God. They were despised as of no value by the world—and they tended to agree with that judgment!—but were precious and beloved in God's eyes. Theirs were lives of humility and obedience, charity and patience; daily they made progress on the path of spiritual life, and they enjoyed God's favor.

These desert hermits stand as an example for all in religious communities. *Their* power to stimulate us to stronger efforts toward perfection ought to be greater than the power of the lukewarm to tempt us toward laziness and self-indulgence.

Consider, finally, the fervor of the religious orders when they were first founded. A splendid devotion to prayer, a rivalry in virtue, an admirable discipline, reverence, and obedience in all things, under the leadership of a superior—all this is evident. The footsteps they left behind bear witness that their members were holy and spiritually perfect, and that they fought the Enemy bravely and conquered the world!

Today, however, the "great" person is merely one who refrains from obvious sins and performs his duties without complaint! How lukewarm and careless we have become in this age! Our original fervor fades quickly, and our laziness makes us tire of life. Let us who have all these examples of true devoutness not "fall asleep" in our pursuit of virtue.

xix. *Some religious practices lead to holiness of life.*
The life of a person who aspires to holiness ought to be marked by every virtue. Such a person will in fact be what he appears to others to be; in other words, what God sees within him ought to be greater than what other people can appreciate. Above all, in everything we do, in every situation of our lives, we should conduct ourselves like the good angels and live in constant reverence of God.

Let us begin each day by renewing our resolutions and our faith, as if this were the first day of our religious commitment, by praying in this manner: *O Lord my God, help me to live according to my resolve to place myself at your service. Grant that on this day I may begin to live without fault; for till now I have not been the person I should have been.*

We shall not make progress unless we desire to do so. And good progress requires a good effort. Yet even a person who has made a strong resolution can expect to make only slow progress; so how can a person who only half-wills to become holy succeed? There are many ways in which our resolve may fail. And even a small lapse from our usual religious practices must be counted a loss of ground.

If you would remain steadfast in your efforts, remember that you are really sustained by the grace of God, not by your own wisdom. Put your trust in him before any undertaking—but remember that though man proposes, God disposes. For God's way is not man's way.

If we occasionally omit some customary act of devotion, for the sake of caring for the needs of another, we do ourselves no harm. But if we simply grow weary and neglect our acts of piety, we harm ourselves grievously. Even though we *try* to be constant to our good resolve, we will often fail in many things. We need a definite plan for ourselves, to help us overcome our chief obstacles. By that plan, we should order our inner and outer lives, because such order helps us make spiritual progress.

If you find it difficult to live always in a state of recollection, make it a practice to set aside a time for meditation at least once a day—in the morning or the evening. Begin each morning with a renewal of your resolution; at the end of each day, examine what you have said, thought, and done since morning. Consider whether you have in some way offended God or those who live and work with you.

Like a soldier, arm yourself against the attacks of the devil. Keep your appetite for food in tight rein, and your other bodily inclinations will then be more easily controlled. Keep yourself from idleness. Occupy your time with reading or writing, praying or meditating, or doing some work on behalf of your community.

Be cautious, however, in imposing bodily penances on yourself; they are not advisable for everyone alike. If you do adopt a personal penance, do not perform it in public. Also, do not let your private devotions keep you away from community prayer. Live the penitential life of your community, and only then allow yourself whatever added mortifications your devotion impels you to.

In this matter of penance, remember that not every penance is suitable for every person. Some forms of penance are suitable for feast days, others for other days. One penance may be suitable for moments when temptation strikes; another, for times when our hearts are at peace; another, for times of sadness; and still another, when we experience joyful closeness to the Lord.

Certainly it is true that the major feasts are appropriate times to renew our efforts to live devoutly and abide by the requirements of our faith; to call on the saints for their intercession; and to renew our resolutions—as if we were shortly to end this life and begin the everlasting feast day. In other words, at holy times of the year we should prepare ourselves, by living more devoutly and conscientiously, as if we were soon to stand before God and be given the reward for our earthly labors. As long as death does not appear imminent, let us consider that we are not yet well prepared for it and are unworthy of the glory that awaits us at the appointed hour. In that manner, let us prepare for death. As we read in the Gospel according to Luke: "Blessed is that servant whom his master, when he shall come, shall find watching. Amen I say to you: he shall make him ruler over all his goods" (12.43-44).

xx. *Learn to love solitude and silence.*

Set aside some suitable times for meditation, and think of the favors that God has granted you. Do not busy your mind about subtle questions. Choose for your reading something that will awaken repentance in your heart rather than stimulate your mind. You will find that you have a great deal of time for quiet meditation if you simply keep away from idle chatter and visits, and from those who love to exchange gossip. It was the practice of many great saints to avoid the presence of others as much as they could, and to serve God in solitude. As one philosopher wrote: "Whenever I have been with others, I have returned less a man" [Seneca, *Epistles* vii]. One commonly finds that this observation is most true when one has participated in lengthy conversations and meetings. It is far easier to remain silent than to keep from saying more than one should. It is likewise far easier to stay at home than to keep oneself in check when in the company of others. If it is our aim to live the spiritual life, we must, like Jesus, go apart from the crowd.

It is true also that until one has learned to love being alone, one cannot be sure of oneself in the company of others. Until one has learned to love silence, one cannot speak well in the presence of others. Just as no one who is unwilling to be ruled can rule well, and no one who is unwilling to obey can govern well, so also no one can know true joy whose conscience troubles him.

The confidence of the saints was always based on their fear of God. Their great virtues and blessings of grace did not prompt them to become careless or proud. It is the wicked person who deceives himself and finds his "security" in pride and arrogance.

It is a mistake, of course, to look for security in this life. Though you may seem to be a "good" person, it may be, as often happens, that you are allowing others' good opinion of you to be the basis of a false self-confidence. Many persons are better off because they frequently are beset by temptations, which keep them from smugness and pride and carelessness in their behavior.

Consider this: if a person could keep from hankering after passing pleasures and worldly business, and put all his trust in God and things divine—things helpful for his soul—what peace of conscience he would enjoy!

A person who has no sorrow for his sins is hardly worthy of Heaven. If you wish to awaken a heartfelt contrition, go aside to a quiet place, shut out the distractions of the world, as Scripture advises: "In your chamber bewail your sins" (Psalm 4.4 [Vulgate]). There you will find what is lost elsewhere. This place of quiet retreat will grow in its appeal for you the more time you spend in it; but you will get little comfort from it if you go there seldom.

It is in silence that the devout soul best advances in virtue and understanding of the truths of Scripture. In silence, the soul cleanses herself in tears of remorse nightly, and thus grows closer to her Creator and escapes the distracting world. God and his holy angels draw near the person whose attention is withdrawn from friends and associates. It is better for us to look after our spiritual needs in solitude than to neglect them in order to work public miracles. It is praiseworthy for a holy person to avoid public gatherings and shun the limelight.

Why should a person who has chosen a religious life wish to experience things not compatible with that life? "The world passes away and the concupiscence thereof" (1 John 2.17). Your sensual appetites sometimes draw you away from your vocation; and when your moment of weakness has passed, what have you to show for it but a heavy conscience and a sadness of heart? What begins happily often has a sad end; a merry evening is often a prelude to a sad dawn. Bodily pleasure always begins sweetly, but finally leads to regret, or even to death.

What is it that one can experience in the world but cannot experience in the cloister? All things on earth and in the heavens are made of the same elements. Everything visible under the sun is subject to change and decay. You may look for satisfaction elsewhere, but you will not find it. If you were able to see all earthly things at once, it would be an empty vision.

Raise your eyes instead to God and ask forgiveness for your sins and failings. Leave worldly things to the worldly, and take to heart the things that God has commanded of you. Close the door that separates you

from the world and call upon Jesus, your Beloved.
Nowhere else will you find such peace as his presence
can give you. If you had never left this place of solitude, idle gossip would not have assailed your ears. It
should not surprise you that, if you hunger after the
latest news, its unpleasantness disturbs your heart.

xxi. *How to awaken sorrow for one's sins.*
Here are the ways to progress in virtue: cultivate in
yourself a proper fear of God; discipline your five
senses; do not seek more liberty than is good for you;
avoid silliness. The sorrow of repentance is the source
of many blessings; carelessness about spiritual things
keeps many blessings from reaching us.

Is it not surprising that *anyone* can know happiness
in this life, which is a life of exile and dangers to the
soul? We go about our lives in lighthearted fashion,
pretending that we have no faults or weaknesses, laugh-
ing mindlessly through the day—when all along we
have good reason to weep. It is a false "liberty" and a
false "joy" that are not grounded on a good conscience
and on a fear of the Lord.

The truly happy person is the one who can set cares
aside and compose his thoughts to consider the bur-
densome weight of sin. Happy also is the person who
shuns anything that might cause him to violate his
conscience. He will struggle with all his strength to
fight bad habit with good.

If you do not unnecessarily involve yourself in the affairs of others, they are more likely to do you the same

favor. In particular, do not meddle in affairs that belong properly to your religious superiors. Keep watch instead on yourself, and save your admonitions for yourself rather than lay them on others. If others do not flatter you with their attentions, do not take offense; instead consider whether you are living in a manner becoming a servant of God, and let any failing in that regard be the basis for your sorrow.

We are generally better off having fewer consolations in this life—especially those that benefit the body. If on the other hand we find that we seldom experience divine consolations, we must consider that the fault is ours. Perhaps we have not an adequate sense of our own failings, or perhaps we are still looking for worldly consolations instead. It is better to think we deserve no consolations from God, because our sins actually merit a punishment. If we were completely repentant of our sins, we would find worldly things distasteful and wearisome.

A holy person finds many things to mourn. Whether he considers himself or his neighbors, he sees that no one can escape suffering in this life. And the more closely he examines the pattern of his own life, the more he grieves. The sins and vices that entangle each of us keep us from contemplation of heavenly things and are the chief reasons why our hearts should be in sorrow. I am sure that if we each thought more often about the pains of Hell or purgatory, we would willingly accept our present troubles and would fear no hardship. If we thought more about our eventual death than about how long our earthly lives will be, we would work harder at amending those lives. But because we keep such thoughts far from our hearts and prefer to involve ourselves in little pleasures, our spiritual life remains cold and dormant; and our poor bodies are full of complaints precisely because our souls are nearly lifeless.

So let us pray fervently to the Lord for the grace of repentance, echoing the words of the prophet: "Feed me, O Lord, with the bread of tears, and give me tears in measure for drink" (Psalm 80.6).

xxii. *How to view the miseries of our human condition.*
Wherever you go, whatever your situation, you will certainly live in misery unless you turn to God. What good does it do to be upset whenever you do not get what you wish? Where is the person who is never disappointed? I am not such a person; nor are you, nor is any human being on earth. Every person—even pope and king—suffers trial and pain.

Let us consider, then, who is happiest in this life. Is it not obvious that they are those willing to suffer for God? The wavering, weak-willed person says, "Look at so-and-so, how rich he is, how great, how mighty." But those who keep their eyes fixed on heavenly goods will see at once that material goods are not really goods at all, but only things possessed for a time and easily lost.

Human happiness on earth therefore does not result from having an abundance of material possessions, but only so much as suffices for one's needs. Life on earth is in itself a trial; the spiritual person sees this clearly, sees the weakness of human nature, and "feels" it as a distaste for his present condition. The person who has progressed far toward spiritual perfection in this life cannot help but find it a nuisance to eat and drink, to sleep and wake, to labor and rest, and to be bound to the physical necessities of earthly existence. Such a person would prefer to be free of them and of sin too. For the same reason, the prophet prayed: "From my necessities, O Lord, deliver me" (Psalm 15.17).

Woe to those who do not recognize their own misery; and even more to those who love this wretched and corruptible life. There are even some who, though they can hardly support themselves from day to day by work or begging, would rather continue living in that manner forever than choose the Kingdom of God. How foolish and untrustworthy are those who have enslaved themselves to material goods and have lost their taste for everything except the comforts of the body! Miserable exiles are they indeed, for they will someday discover the worthlessness of everything they have lusted after.

The saints and friends of Christ, on the other hand, did not give themselves to pleasing the body or to aping current fashions. Their hope and aim were to seek the good things that last forever. They directed their lives toward things invisible, things everlasting; for they knew that love of visible things tended to drag them down.

So let us not lose confidence in pursuing the spiritual life. There is still time to make progress; our hour has not yet passed. Let us delay no more, but stand and proclaim: *Now is the time to act, now is the time to fight, and now is the time to amend my life.*

When troubles come your way, then can you gain merit. In other words, before you can come to the place of refreshment, you must pass through fire and water. You cannot overcome the weakness of your nature except by taking complete charge of yourself. So long as we continue to live in our mortal bodies, we will not be free of sin or suffering. We would gladly have a rest from our miseries, but by our sins we lost both innocence and true blessedness. So we must wait patiently until God, in his mercy, frees us from our sinfulness and our mortality.

How frail is our human nature, which is so inclined toward evil. Today you confess your sins; tomorrow, you commit the same sins again. One moment you resolve to be steadfast; the next, you behave as if you had made no resolution. It is not without reason that we should admit our weakness and, in humility, our many failings. Whatever we have by our hard efforts accomplished with the help of God's grace can quickly be lost by a little negligence. We have to wonder what will become of us if we grow lukewarm so readily. If we presume that we enjoy spiritual peace and security, when actually our lives are not holy at all, we put ourselves in grave danger. Perhaps what we need to do is become again as novices in the spiritual life and be instructed anew in holiness, so that we can resolve to amend our lives and make better spiritual progress in the future.

xxiii. *How we should think about death.*

Before long, your life on earth will end; you should therefore give thought to what awaits you elsewhere. Today we live, and tomorrow we die and are quickly forgotten. A person would have to be both dull and hard of heart to think only of the present instead of being more concerned about what is to come.

You will be wise to act and think as though you were to die this very day. If your conscience is at ease, you will not fear death much. Certainly, it is far better to avoid sin than to live in constant fear of death. If today you are not prepared to die, what of tomorrow? Tomorrow may or may not come; for how can you be sure that you will live till tomorrow?

A long life may seem a blessing; but how can it be so if a person does little to amend the way he lives? A long life may in fact not be to one's advantage; it may only provide more time to accumulate guilt. Would that any of us lived truly well for a single day! Many a person looks back over a long life as a Christian believer and sees no spiritual growth. Instead of fearing death, perhaps one would be wiser to consider a long life more dangerous. The person who keeps the prospect of death in mind and prepares for it daily is properly called blessed.

If you ever see anyone die, give thought to the fact that you too will leave this life through the same door.

Each morning, call to mind the possibility that you will not live till sunset; and each evening, do not promise yourself the dawn. Live prepared, therefore, so that death does not catch you unprepared. Many persons die suddenly, unexpectedly; for it is in "the unexpected hour" that the Son of Man will come. When your last moments come, your past life will suddenly look much different to you; and you will be overwhelmed by a feeling of regret for what you failed to do with it.

If a person tries to make his life today to be what he would want it to have been at the moment of his death, he will be both happy and prudent. If he puts material things aside as of no lasting value, sets his mind to improving in virtue and in love for self-discipline and penance, and endures all hardships for the sake of Christ, he will indeed have prepared himself for a happy death.

So too, when you are in good health, you have the opportunity for many good works; but when sickness strikes, what can you do? Just as those who make many pilgrimages seldom become holy, those who are sick seldom become better persons as a result.

Do not put the welfare of your soul in the hands of friends and relatives, nor in other ways put off your spiritual welfare till a later date. Others will forget you faster than you suppose. Take it upon yourself now to accumulate some merit in advance of your need, rather than hoping that others will come to your aid. If you take no care of your spiritual state now, who will worry about it when you are gone?

You see, then, how precious are today's passing moments. *These* are the days in which you achieve your salvation; *now* is the "acceptable time." It is sad to see someone wasting time that could have been spent in a better way. The day will come when you will wish you had just one more day or hour in which to amend your life. And then, will you have it?

What I am saying, dear friend, is that you can save yourself from both a great danger and a fear of death, if you keep the prospect of your own death before your mind. By trying now to live as you should, you will greet your death with a glad heart. By learning to die to the world now, you learn to live now with Christ. By freeing yourself from attachment to worldly things, you are free to go to him. Subject your body to discipline now, and you can face the future life with confidence.

How utterly foolish it is for someone to seek to have a long life when he or she may not even have the present day! How many people are taken by surprise and snatched from this life without warning! We have all heard of people dying suddenly, unexpectedly—by drowning, by falling from a scaffold, in fire, at meal or play, by stabbing, from plague, or at the hands of robbers. Death comes for every person—and, like a shadow, passes quickly.

Have you considered who will remember you after your death, and who will pray for you? Much better, my friend, to look after your spiritual condition now yourself; for you do not even know your fate after death. Store up lasting riches for yourself now, while you can, and do not neglect your own salvation. How? By caring only for the things of God, by honoring the saints of God and winning their friendship, and by imitating their virtues, so that they will be waiting to welcome you into your everlasting home.

Live in this life as a stranger to earth, a pilgrim passing through to another life, and keep your heart free and turned toward God. For here, you have no lasting home. Offer daily to God your prayers, your sighs, your hopes, that your spirit may one day pass into the happiness the Lord has promised those who believe in him.

xxiv. *Anticipate the Lord's Judgment.*

In all the activities of your life, keep your final destiny in mind: consider, that is, how you will stand before the strict Judge from whom nothing is hidden. He will judge you according to the norms of justice; bribes and excuses have no influence on him. How will you, a wretched and foolish sinner, be able to face such a Judge—who knows all your sins—when you cannot bear the wrath of an angry man? Would it not be prudent to prepare yourself for that day of judgment when nothing will be "excused" and no one else can speak on your behalf? Only in this life will your work be spiritually profitable, your remorse acceptable, your petitions heard, and your repentance effective and purifying.

The patient person thoroughly cleanses himself when he grieves more for the malice of the one who does him harm than for the pain it causes him; when he prays for his enemies and sincerely forgives them; when he is quick to apologize for his trespasses; when he tends more toward pity than toward anger; and when he firmly subdues his appetites and subjects his body to his spirit.

Far better to mortify ourselves in this life and free ourselves from evil habits than to be "purged" of our imperfections in the life hereafter. How easily we delude ourselves about how we cater to our bodies. The more we spare ourselves now and the more we pamper our bodily needs, the harder will be that purgation by fire. Our sins will but provide the fuel for the flames.

For those parts of our body by which we have sinned will be severely punished. The lazy person may be driven by red-hot prongs; the glutton may experience indescribable hunger and thirst; the wanton, lustful person may be immersed in burning pitch and foul-smelling brimstone; and the envious may howl like mad dogs. Every vice also will have its own suitable punishment. The proud will wander in total confusion; the greedy will lack every comfort. One hour of punishment in the next life will be like a hundred years of abject penance in this. Here, we have the consolations of friendship, of times of rest. But the condemned have no consolations, no rest.

I urge you strongly, therefore, to repent of your sins now rather than later, and prepare yourself to live forever with the blessed. For when that day comes, you will be free of those who caused you grief in this life;

and you will stand in judgment of those to whom you now submit out of obedience. In that day, the poor and humble will be affirmed, and the proud will cower in fear. Then, at last, those who were fools for Christ in this world will be seen to have been truly wise.

In that day too, every trial that we endured patiently will seem pleasing in remembrance, and the voices of evil will be stilled; the devout will have their hearts gladdened, while the irreligious will grieve; and the body that was mortified will be more satisfied than the body pampered in every way. The plain garment will seem rich, the luxurious one faded and tattered; the lowly cottage will be more highly praised than the palace of gold. In that day, patient perseverance will be seen to be more powerful than all the powers of this world; a ready obedience will be esteemed above any human cleverness; an honest conscience will gladden the heart more than profound learning; and freedom from riches will be seen as a jewel more valuable than any earthly treasure.

When that day comes for you, you will take more satisfaction from having prayed devoutly than from having dined elegantly; from having preferred silence and solitude to gossip and talkativeness. You will see that your good works were of far more value than all your fine talk, and your hardest penances will please you more than any of the pleasures that earth has to offer.

It makes much more sense to endure our little troubles now rather than have to suffer far worse in the next life. Now is the time to test what you can bear hereafter. If a little pain is all you can tolerate now, how would you be able to endure everlasting pain? If minor annoyances make you irritable now, what will Hell's fires do to you? You cannot have it both ways: the pleasures of this life, and afterward the reward of Christ's kingdom.

If your life on earth has been a succession of honors and pleasures, what good would they be to you if you should die this day? One who is mired in sin and its pleasures does well to fear death and judgment.

You see, therefore, that except for loving God and serving him alone, everything in this life is a snare and a delusion. On the other hand, if you do love God with all your heart, you have no reason to fear death or judgment or the punishment of Hell—for perfect love assures that you will be welcomed by God. If as yet your love for God is imperfect and does not wholly keep you from sin, but your fear of Hell does motivate you to avoid sin, that is good. It is proper to have a fear of God's judgment. The person who altogether lacks such fear cannot continue long in God's grace but will soon become a servant to the devil.

xxv. *Make a determined effort to amend your life.*
Be watchful. Give yourself diligently to the works of God. Think often of your decision to follow Christ and leave worldly concerns behind you. Was it not your intention to dedicate yourself to God and grow in holiness? Make spiritual perfection your goal, then, be-

cause before too long you will receive the reward of your efforts; and neither fear nor sorrow will fill your heart at the moment of your death.

Exert yourself now, and soon you will find rest—in fact, unending joy. If you remain faithful in your intention, God will prove faithful and generous in rewarding you. Do not lose heart; do not despair of your salvation. But do not assume either that you are already entitled to God's favor; or you will become lazy and proud.

Let me tell you a parable.

There was once a man who wavered anxiously between hopefulness and despair; and his heart was sad. He knelt before the altar of a church, and his thoughts were these: "I wish I knew whether I should continue this struggle . . . day after day . . ." At that, he heard God's answer: *If you had the answer to your question, what would you do? You will have peace of mind if you do exactly that now.* The man's mind was suddenly at peace, and he decided to do what God asked of him. All anxiety left him. He was no longer curious about what the future held for him. He decided to look upon his every good work as God's will for him.

It is as the prophet said: "Trust in the Lord and do good; dwell in the land and you will feed on its riches" (Psalm 37.3).

What keeps many from deciding to work at improving themselves is simply the sheer difficulty of it, the demands of the battle. Yet it is always the case that the person who tries to overcome the worst difficulties or leap the highest hurdles is the one who surpasses others—in virtue as in other things. The way to make the most spiritual progress and gain the most grace is to win the hardest battles over your selfishness and willfulness. It is true that each person has special difficulties to overcome; but anyone who is sincere and persistent will make much more progress over even strong passions than someone who is even-tempered but less concerned about his spiritual health.

There are basically two ways in which you can improve yourself. First, take yourself away from those vices toward which our weak nature inclines us. Second, pray hardest for the graces you most need.

Further, try to overcome in yourself those faults which most annoy you when you meet them in other persons. Make the best of others' good example, and look for every opportunity to imitate it. At the same time, do not yourself be guilty of behavior that you complain about in others, or at least work to correct your own behavior as soon as possible. Others observe your behavior, just as you observe theirs!

Religious persons who are fervent, well mannered, and self-disciplined are pleasant to live with. But it is painful to watch people lost in their own depravity, hypocrites who do not practice what they profess to believe. It causes much harm when people abandon their proper vocations and involve themselves in things for which they have neither a talent nor a mandate.

Recall to yourself your own spiritual resolution, and keep before your mind the image of Jesus crucified. You can measure your progress, even after many years of pilgrimage toward God, by placing a crucifix before you, and asking yourself whether this image does not make you ashamed that you have not become more Christlike. A Christian believer who meditates attentively on the holy life of Jesus, especially his passion and death, will learn all that anyone needs to know about spiritual goods. We can have no better guide than Jesus. If he were truly to live in our hearts, how quickly and completely we would learn!

Devout believers will willingly accept and do everything that Jesus asks of them. Those who are but lukewarm in their faith and behavior will find their lives one trial after another; they will lack all spiritual consolations, and know that they are forbidden to seek the consolations the world has to offer. In the same way, one who has adopted religious life and does not live according to the rule of his community is very likely to jeopardize his spiritual welfare; in his hunger for freedom, he leads himself into troubles of his own making; and his expectations will constantly be frustrated.

How is it that those living in cloister can even manage to get along with each other? In this way: they seldom leave the cloister; they dedicate themselves to contemplative prayer; they eat but meager foods; they wear coarse clothing; they work hard, speak seldom, spend long hours at prayer, and read frequently; they impose various kinds of self-discipline. The Carthusians and Cistercians, for example, rise every night to sing the Lord's praise. It is therefore hard to excuse spiritual sluggishness in ourselves when we consider that so many others have shown us the way to praise God.

If you had nothing else to concern yourself with but praising God, if you never had to eat, drink, or sleep, if you spent all your time looking after your spiritual needs, you would be a much happier person than you are now. Now, you are a slave to the needs of your body. One could well wish to be free of such needs and concentrate instead on finding refreshment for one's soul; for that is what we too seldom experience.

It is only when a person reaches the stage where he seeks no comfort from any created thing that he begins to enjoy God instead. Such a person knows true contentment, no matter what may befall him in this life. He will neither rejoice at his good fortune nor grieve over his wants, but will place himself entirely in God's care. In his mind, God is all important; all existing things live in God and never perish, but only serve his plan for his creation.

So I say again: always keep in mind the reason why you exist. Time lost is never regained. Unless you care enough to seek it, you will never acquire virtue. If you relax your efforts and become lukewarm, you will fall into evil habits. But if you work to become more devout, you will find peace, and your hardships will weigh lightly on you because of God's helping grace and your own love for what is virtuous. A holy person is truly prepared for anything.

Experience shows us that it is more difficult to resist our own vices and passions than to sweat at hard labor. We are therefore much better off overcoming our minor faults than having to do battle with faults that have been allowed to grow worse.

You will, then, always be content when evening comes if you have put the day to good use. Keep watch over your actions; be alert, on guard yourself, and, no matter what others may choose for themselves, do not neglect your own spiritual welfare. In particular, the more closely you restrain your natural appetites, the more progress you will make in the spiritual life.

Amen.

Book Two

The Imitation of Christ

BOOK TWO

The Interior Life

i. *Prepare your heart for union with Christ.*
THE LORD says, "The Kingdom of God is within you" (Luke 17.21). Turn your whole heart toward God, therefore, and forsake this heartless world. In that way, you will find rest for your soul. Place no value on external things; pay attention instead to what is within you. You will then see the kingdom of God taking shape within you. This is a kingdom of peace and joy, two gifts of the Holy Spirit that are not given to sinners.

Christ will come to you, offering you his consolation, if you make your heart into a fit dwelling for him. The hidden beauty and glory of your heart are what delight him. He visits often the heart of one whose interior self is well prepared to receive him. His sweet and consoling presence brings great peace and wonderful intimacy.

Be therefore like a faithful bride preparing yourself—that is, your heart—for the coming of this Bridegroom. As he has promised: "If any one loves me, he will keep my word, and we will come to him and make our abode with him" (John 14.23). Make room for Christ, but deny all others entrance. If you have Christ, you need no other wealth. He will provide for your needs, and supply your wants, so that you need not depend on the fickleness of human assistance. Christ remains ever true to his word, and stands beside us till death comes for us.

No matter how helpful and friendly others are toward you, do not place much confidence in them. Nor should it upset you greatly if others oppose or contradict you. Those who support us today may be our enemies tomorrow—and vice versa. For human beings are changeable, like the wind. Place your trust entirely in God; fear and love only him. He will defend you. He will do whatever is best for you.

You have no lasting home here on earth. Here, you are a stranger, a pilgrim, wherever you may be. You will have no lasting rest till you are united completely with Christ.

So why look for any comfort or reward in this world? This is not the place where you will find what you seek. Keep your eye fixed instead on Heaven, and glance on earthly things only to recall that they will *all* pass away—and you with them. Avoid clinging to material things; they can trap you and lead you to perdition. Keep God foremost in your thoughts, instead, and pray constantly to Christ.

If you do not know how to meditate on the things of Heaven, begin by calling to mind the passion of Christ and looking upon his blessed wounds. By meditating devoutly on the wounds of Christ, especially his precious stigmata, you will find that your own sufferings will bring you a kind of comfort, that the opinion your enemies have of you will not bother you, and that the lies they tell about you will not disturb you.

When Christ was in this world, many people despised and hated him. When he most needed help, his friends deserted him as if they scorned his company. Yet he was willing to suffer and be despised. So how is it that we can complain of anything? He had enemies, and many of them libeled him. So why should we expect everyone to be friendly toward us and assist us when we need help? How can anyone be a friend of Christ yet be always looking for ways to avoid hardship? How can our patience deserve any reward if we are never tested? No, we must suffer with Christ if we would reign with him.

If only you had just once been perfectly united with Christ, or had a small taste of his love, you would forget all about your own comfort and welcome the enmity of others. To love Christ is to know how little one deserves to be loved. A person who loves Christ, also loves truth. Such a one has a well-developed spiritual life and is in charge of his emotions and appetites. Such a one can turn to God at any moment and, by rising above himself, be filled with spiritual peace. The key is to see this life as it really is—not as common opinion thinks it is—and live according to God's wisdom rather than man's.

To live an "interior life" means to place a relatively low value on this world's goods. It means not waiting for special times and places before turning to God in prayers and devotions. A person who has progressed in the spiritual life has learned how to recollect his thoughts whenever he pleases; his attention is not distracted by this and that. He is not a slave to work or to "business that can't wait." He performs whatever work is required of him, and accepts events as they come. When others behave unexpectedly or wickedly, he remains steadfast; for he has learned to govern well his own behavior. The more a person gets himself involved in external affairs, the more likely he is to be upset and distracted by the actions of others.

In your own case, if you were entirely free from sin, everything you do would be for your good and your profit. But because you are not entirely free of worldly concerns, and because your selfishness is not yet entirely set aside, you will continue to be upset and disturbed about many things. The one thing most likely to lead a person into wickedness is a greedy attachment to created things. On the other hand, if you can deny yourself the desire for material comforts, you will be able to give close thought to things pertaining to Heaven and thus frequently experience an interior joy.

ii. *Humility means placing one's trust in God.*
Instead of worrying about who is for you and who is against you, keep God beside you in everything you do.

If your conscience is clear, God will protect you. Even the most malicious person cannot harm one whom God desires to help. You will be assured of God's help if you have learned to suffer in silence. God surely knows when and how to "free" you, so place yourself confidently in his care. It is God's work to deliver us and free us from our distress.

We are often better off for having others know of our faults, and for having our faults criticized: we grow in humility as a result. The person who humbly acknowledges his faults thereby silences his critics and defuses the enmity of his associates.

God protects only humble persons; it is the humble whom he frees, loves, and consoles. He watches after them and disposes numerous graces on them. In their moments of humiliation, he raises them up and calls them to his glory. To the humble he reveals his secrets and offers his invitations to come to him. That is why humble persons know peace despite their many troubles; their trust is in God, not in the world. So too, you should consider that you have made good progress in the spiritual life only when the esteem you have for yourself is less than the esteem you have for others.

iii. *Avoid hypocrisy in your dealings with others.*
You will no doubt agree that a person who is not at peace with himself can hardly bring peace to others. Of two men, one peaceful and the other learned, the peaceful man accomplishes the most good. A sensual man, on the other hand, not only makes everything, even good things, evil by his touch, but is always ready

to believe any evil about another. The peaceful man, being also a good man, spreads goodness wherever he goes.

If a person's spirit is at ease, he is not forever suspecting the worst of others. The restless spirit is constantly being disturbed by suspicions; he knows no peace, and allows others no peace either. He reveals what should be kept secret and neglects his own responsibilities. He watches to see that others behave as they should but neglects his own duties.

Examine your own behavior first of all; and then perhaps you will be entitled to be zealous about the behavior of your acquaintances. You may find that you are constantly offering excuses for yourself that you would not accept from them. As a rule, justice is always better served if we accuse ourselves and excuse others. If we wish others to bear with us, we should bear with them. Examine how far you are from being a person of true charity and humility. If you were such a person, you wouldn't think of being angry at another; no, you would save all your indignation for yourself!

It is no accomplishment to be able to get along with kind and gentle persons; they are pleasant to be with. Because we all prefer a peaceful life, we prefer to be among persons whose habits are like our own. What requires much grace is to live at peace with rude and unholy persons, with selfish and irritating persons. That is a noble and praiseworthy effort.

There are those who get along well with others and are themselves at peace; others lack peace in them-

selves, never bring it to others, and are a burden to
everyone—perhaps most of all to themselves. A small
number live at peace with themselves and also try to
help others know the same peace in their own lives.

What many do not understand is that, in this life of
misery, they can find interior peace in only one way:
not by freeing themselves from suffering, but by accepting it patiently and humbly. It is knowing how to
suffer that enables some to live at peace with themselves; they, having conquered themselves, are the
masters of the world, friends of Christ, and heirs of
Heaven.

iv. *Be steadfast in following the ways of God.*

A person rises above preoccupation with material
goods on the wings of simplicity and purity of life. He
has but one goal (God), and all his desires are therefore
holy. Simplicity leads him to God, and purity of life
enables him to enjoy being in God's presence.

If you have taught your heart to seek only what is
good, no good deed will be an effort for you. If you use
your life to please God and care for the welfare of your
neighbor, you will experience the inner freedom of the
just. For if your heart is rightly taught, then every creature, no matter how small or insignificant it may seem,
will show you something of God's goodness. The pure
of heart see and understand all things as they are, for
their hearts can see as far as Heaven and Hell. A person
judges the outside world according to the kind of person he is on the inside. If this world offers any joy, the

pure of heart experience it. Those whose consciences are deformed know pain and anguish all too well.

A piece of old iron, when cast into a furnace, soon loses its rust and becomes white-hot. In the same way, if a person turns completely toward God, all his old sluggishness falls from him and he becomes a new person. But if a person relaxes his efforts, every discomfort and self-sacrifice seems to him a burden. It is only when a person works at bringing himself under control and at walking conscientiously along the path to God that all those once-difficult things come to seem less of a hindrance.

v. *Consider often what progress you have made in spiritual growth.*

No one should think he can always be his own best advisor; for all of us commonly are deficient in grace and wisdom. The small amount of "inner light" we are born with is soon lost through our negligence. And then we do not see that our hearts are actually blind. At the same time, when we sin, we make matters worse by trying to excuse ourselves. We mistake our passions for zeal, berate others for minor faults, and fail to see the worse faults in ourselves. How quick we are to feel, and brood over, our own sufferings while caring not at all about the sufferings we cause others. Anyone who weighed his own behavior accurately would have little reason to condemn the behavior of others.

But if we take care first of our spiritual lives and mend and improve them constantly, we will be less inclined to gossip about others. If you cannot hold still about what others do or don't do, and if you neglect your own responsibilities, you will fail to become devout at heart. If you keep your attention fixed on God and on yourself, you will not be troubled by what you see in others.

If you give no thought to your own spiritual state, what do you think about? And after you have spent time at other things, how have you gained any benefit if you spent that time without regard to your own spiritual needs? It is much the best course to keep your one goal always in mind, your own interior condition always before your eyes; and set all else aside, if you would know peace of mind.

That is why I recommend that you keep yourself free of worry about temporary things that pass away; such entanglement is a serious mistake, for it keeps you from making good progress in spiritual things. What we need to learn is that there is nothing great or high or pleasing or desirable except God and the things of God. The benefits that created things can offer you are really distractions that draw us toward vanity; the soul who loves God scorns those inferior things that draw us away from him. Only God, who is eternal and infinite, can satisfy all our needs, comfort our souls, and bring true joy to our bodies.

vi. *If you would be happy, keep your conscience alert.*
A good person is rewarded by the approval of his own well-formed conscience. Keep your conscience honed,

and your happiness will be undisturbed. A well-formed conscience can not only help you through difficulties but can even bring you joy despite them. It is the ill-formed conscience that makes a person nervous and unsettled.

If your conscience—the voice of your heart—does not reproach you, your sleep will be restful. But unless you have lived in harmony with your conscience, do not congratulate yourself. The sinner never experiences inner joy or peace; for as the Lord says, "There is no peace for the wicked" (Isaiah 48.22). Even if others should boast, saying "We are happy; nothing can happen to take our happiness from us, and no one dares to harm us," pay no attention to them. God's anger will rise to deal with such persons; their lives will come to nothing, and their ideas will pass away.

The person who truly loves God does not find it difficult to welcome suffering and difficulties; for such love gets its strength from the cross of the Lord. The praise that others offer us is short-lived; and the consolations that the world can offer us are always accompanied by sorrow. The good person receives his reward from his conscience, not from the lips of others; his joy is from and in God; his happiness is founded on Truth. Such a person, who desires the glory that lasts forever, is not interested in the passing fame this world can offer. On the other hand, those for whom worldly fame is important, or who do not scorn it heartily, can care little for the glory of Heaven.

Only the person who pays no attention to the praise or blame that others give him will experience peace of heart; and the integrity of his conscience will reward him with interior contentment and quiet. For after all, praise adds nothing to your holiness, and blame takes nothing away from it. You are what you are; and you are no better than what God sees in you. If you care about that, you will not care what people say about you. They see only the appearances; God sees the heart. They see only what was done; God sees the motive.

It is a sign of spiritual humility to do good always, without thought of reward. It is a mark of deep faith and great purity to avoid seeking consolation from material things. The person who is not busy trying to justify himself to himself has obviously entrusted himself to God. As St. Paul said, "It is not the one who recommends himself who is approved, but the one whom the Lord recommends" (2 Corinthians 10.18).

To walk with God in spirit and to keep free of attachment to externals—this is the desire of anyone who wishes to live the interior life.

vii. *Let Jesus dwell in your heart.*
It is a great blessing to understand what it means to love Jesus and to despise oneself for his sake. Set aside all your other affections so that you can love him; for he asks that we love him alone above all else. The affection we have for other human beings is colored by insincerity and may falter; but Jesus' love for us is faithful and lasting. To attach oneself to a frail creature is to fall when it falls. To attach oneself to Jesus is to take strength from him.

Love Jesus as your friend. He will not leave you, as

human friends may. Nor will he let you suffer an ever-lasting death. The time is coming, whether you like it or not, when you will have to leave all your earthly possessions behind. So you are well advised to attach yourself to Jesus in this life till the moment of your death. Look for the glory that he can give you when no one else will be able to help you.

As your Beloved, he expects from you not what belongs to others but your own heart. He wants to be the lord of your heart; but he cannot be enthroned there till you have freed yourself from affection for material things.

The trust you place in others (except for Jesus) will almost always lead to disappointment. Do not become dependent on, or place all your confidence in, a fellow human being; for "all flesh is grass" (Isaiah 15.6) and, like the flower of grass, will eventually fade away.

How easy it is to be deceived by what others seem to be, and how often one is disappointed when one looks to them for comfort or assistance. On the other hand, if we look to Jesus to give us what we need, he will be there to help us. He who seeks himself finds only himself—and is soon ruined. In fact, he who does not seek Jesus does himself much more harm than his enemies and all the world could do him.

viii. *Live in friendship with Jesus.*
We find that when we are close to Jesus, we are happy and nothing seems difficult for us. When we are not close to him, our lives become a burden to us. If we lack

the interior comfort Jesus can bring us, we find no lasting comfort from others; one word from him brings us full consolation. Mary Magdalen ceased her weeping immediately when Martha said to her, "The Master has come and is asking to see you" (John 11.28). It is always a happy experience to hear Jesus call one from sorrow to a joyful spirit.

Consider how "dry and hard" you are apart from Jesus, how vain and foolish your behavior when you seek after anything but him! Do you really think it a greater loss to lose Jesus than to lose the whole world? Do you see anything the world can give you that Jesus cannot? Compared to the sweet paradise of living in friendship with him, life without him is a constant Hell. If Jesus is with you, none can harm you.

The person who finds Jesus discovers a great treasure, more valuable than any earthly good; and the person who loses him loses more than all worldly goods combined. To live without Jesus is to be poorer than the poor; but no earthly treasure can compare with the wealth of one who lives in his grace.

It is the best art to know how to talk with Jesus, and the highest wisdom to remain close to him. If you are a humble and peaceful person, Jesus will dwell within you. If you are a devout and composed person, he will remain with you. But if you turn to the world for your happiness, you will lose his grace and close your heart to him. And if you do that, where will you turn, and who will then be your friend? We all need friendship; and if Jesus is not our best friend, we condemn ourselves to sadness and isolation. It is so very foolish for us to place our trust or seek our joy in another person. It is much better to have the whole world hate you rather than do anything to harm your friendship with Jesus. Of all those who are dear to you, give him the highest place in your heart. Love all others for his sake, but love him for himself alone.

There is a reason why Jesus should be loved in that way. He alone, of all your friends, is entirely good and faithful. Because of your love for him, you must love both your friends and enemies alike; and you must pray to him that all persons will come to know and love him.

Let Jesus dwell with you as your friend, as he does with every good person. Do not look to others for any special praise or esteem; for only God, who has no equal, deserves more than ordinary love. Do not wish that anyone show any special love toward you; nor do you show any such love to another. Keep yourself free from worldly attachments, so that you can bring to God a pure and open heart and thus find how sweeet the Lord is. This is a blessing that you could never have except that God's grace prepares you and draws you to unite yourself with him alone.

With the help of God's grace, we can do anything; if we lose his grace, we become impoverished and weak—abandoned by ourselves, so to speak, to sorrow. Yet if that should happen to us, we should not wrap ourselves in sadness and despair. No, we should patiently await God's will for us, ready to accept it on behalf of Jesus Christ—remembering that after winter comes summer, and after night, the day, and after a storm, the calm.

ix. *Do not be a seeker after comfort.*
If we enjoy God's favor, it is easy to free ourselves from attachment to human consolations. The best course of all to follow is to be able to live without any conforting, from God or from man, and to accept this place of exile for our hearts in honor of God. That course requires that we do not seek self-satisfaction in anything or worry about what we "deserve."

It hardly matters whether one is cheerful and devout at the moment when God's grace comes. That is a moment anyone might desire, for God's grace makes this earthly journey easy. We can hardly be surprised that our lives do not seem a burden to us when we feel borne along by the Almighty, the Supreme Guide. It would be unnatural for us not to enjoy such a consolation; for we know what a burden our selfishness is to us. The holy martyr Saint Lawrence, accompanied by his priest, conquered the world because he hated everything in it that pleased him. And because he loved Christ, he was able to accept patiently the death of Sixtus, God's high priest, his companion whom he loved dearly. Lawrence's love for his Creator made it possible for him to place less importance on his love for man. He preferred God's good pleasure to having the continued consolation of a human friendship. You too must prepare yourself to part with a close and dear friend out of love for God. Nor should you be overly grieved when you are dropped by one whom you considered a friend; for eventually we must all be parted from one another.

It is a long and hard struggle to learn to master oneself and set oneself on the path toward God. If one trusts in oneself only, one soon yearns for some human reward. One who truly loves Christ and pursues virtue does not stop to be refreshed by human comforts or bodily pleasures; rather, he welcomes severe trials and difficult obstacles for the sake of his friendship with Christ.

Whenever you find yourself blessed by God with some spiritual consolation, accept it gratefully. Remember, though, that such a blessing is purely a gift; you did not deserve it. Do not prance about with joy and become presumptuous of receiving further blessings; instead, let the gift encourage you to greater humility, and guard your behavior more closely, for the hour of elation will pass and temptation will follow.

So too, when the spiritual consolation fades, do not despair of receiving another; wait in all humility, and with patience, for the next heavenly visitation, when God will restore and increase the comfort he offers you. This pattern would not seem so strange to you if you knew God's ways better. Rapid changes in fortune were common in the lives of the great saints and prophets of old. One such person, recalling a moment when he was blessed by grace, said: "In my prosperity I said, 'I shall never be disturbed' " (Psalm 30.7). But when the grace was taken away, his feelings were quite different: "When you hid your face, I was troubled" (30.8). Instead of despairing, he prayed more earnestly to the Lord: "To you, O Lord, I cried out. I shall plead with my God" (30.9). At last, his prayer bore fruit; and he testified that he was heard: "The Lord has heard me and has had pity on me; the Lord is my helper" (30.11). And what was the help? "You changed my sorrow into joy and wound me around with gladness" (30.12).

If such is the experience of the saints, all the more reason for us, weak and needy as we are, to remain hopeful despite being sometimes warm with spiritual fervor and other times cold. The Spirit comes and goes according to his will. The saintly Job said of God's dealing with man: "You observe him at the start of each day, and you put him to the test without warning" (Job 7.18).

Why should I place my hope or trust in anyone besides God and his great mercy and heavenly grace? Even if I live among good persons, devout brethren, faithful friends, holy books, edifying manuscripts, and agreeable songs and hymns—as I do—I can find little pleasure in them when I feel abandoned by God's grace and left to my own poor wits. At such times, I have found no better cure than to be patient and resign myself to accept God's will for me.

I have never met anyone—no matter how devout or religious—who has not experienced at some time a complete withdrawal of grace and a drying up of fervor. Every saint who experienced a sublime rapture of enlightenment also experienced temptation beforehand and afterward. I therefore do not see how anyone could be called worthy of the full contemplation of God if he has not suffered willingly some tribulation as God's will. Temptation, in fact, is usually a sign of a coming consolation from Heaven; for such consolation has been promised to anyone tested by temptation. Our Lord said, "To the one who is victorious, I shall give to eat of the Tree of Life" (Revelation 2.7). The consolation of God is given to strengthen us against adversity; and temptation follows to keep us from taking a spiritual pride in any good we may have done with the assistance of grace.

The devil sleeps not; the flesh is not yet dead. So do not cease your preparations for battle. On your right and on your left, you have enemies who are constantly on watch.

x. *Give thanks always for God's favors to you.*
You were born to work; so why should you look for ways to escape it? Teach yourself to be patient rather than to seek your own comfort; learn to carry your cross willingly rather than look for what pleases you. There is not a single person in the world who would not gladly trade all earthly and bodily pleasures for a chance at spiritual consolation and joy. Things that please the body are either a vanity or a vice. Spiritual joys, which are the fruit of virtue and the gift of God to holy souls, are pleasing and noble.

Because we live with the prospect of temptation constantly before us, and because too much self-confidence and self-indulgence keep us from experiencing a respite from temptation, we are not quite free to enjoy God's blessings as much as we wish. God's free gift of consoling grace sometimes meets with our (evil) reluctance to offer back the gift with our thanks. How can the gifts of grace flow in us if we are ungrateful to the Giver? Ought we not return them with thanks to the Fountainhead? God always gives his grace to those who are properly grateful for them. That which God intends for the humble he will take away from the proud.

I do not look for any consolation that makes me think I have no need for repentance. I do not wish to learn an art of contemplation that leads me to pride. I know that not everything lofty is holy; not everything sweet is good for me to eat; not every desire is pure; and not everything I hold dear is pleasing to God. What I do look for, and accept willingly, is the grace by which I can become more humble and repentant, more willing to say no to myself.

A person who has learned from the gift of grace and the lash of its withdrawal is not likely to give himself much credit, but will instead be likely to admit that, in himself, he is poor and empty. We must give to God what is God's, and count as our own what is truly ours. Let us then give him thanks for his grace, and accept the blame and punishment we each deserve for our faults.

If you always seek the lowest place for yourself, the highest will be given you; for the highest cannot exist apart from the lowest. The saintly persons who are holiest in God's sight are the ones who regard themselves as the least of his servants. The more their hearts are humble, the more glorious they are. They do not thirst for worldly glory; they are already filled with truth and heavenly glory. Recognizing that God is the one who supports and strengthens them, they see no reason to be proud. Any good they have received, they look to God as the giver of it. The only glory they seek is what God can give them. They desire that God be praised, through themselves and through all his saints. Their lives have no other purpose.

If you are grateful for even the least of God's gifts to you, you will make yourself worthy to receive a greater gift. Look upon even the smallest gift, however insignificant, as if it were the greatest gift you could receive. Each gift *is* special; for, when you consider the dignity of the Giver, how could any gift from him be thought small or worthless? So also, when he gives us trials and sufferings, accept them as things we need for our spiritual welfare. Everything God allows to happen to us is for our good.

Be grateful, therefore, when God's grace is given to you, and be patient when it is withdrawn. Pray for its return then; and be watchful and humble, lest your behavior cause you to lose it again.

xi. *Do not shun the cross of Jesus.*
Many look forward to the heavenly kingdom of Jesus, but few are willing to carry his cross. Many Christians wish to have his consolations, but few willingly accept

the trials he sends them. Many accept the invitation to join him at table, but few are ready to join him in fasting. Everyone desires to be happy with him, but no one desires to suffer anything for his sake. Many follow after him for the breaking of the bread, but how few are those who are just as ready to drink from the chalice of his passion. Many are impressed by his miracles, but few approach the shameful cross. Many are quite ready to love him so long as no hardship is required of them; many praise him and bless him so long as they enjoy *his* blessings. But if Jesus leaves them for a time and "goes into hiding," they are quick to complain or to lapse into a sour mood.

Yet there are those who love Jesus for his own sake, and not because he brings them any comfort; they bless him despite their troubles and sorrows, just as they do when they feel his comforting grace. They would go on praising him and offering him their thanks even if he never rewarded them with spiritual consolations. Such is the power of a love for Jesus that is untainted by self-ishness.

Surely those persons who look to Jesus only for the consolations he can give them deserve to be called mercenaries? Are they not showing that they love themselves more than they love Christ? Is there, in fact, any person whose one purpose is to serve God without the slightest concern for his own advantage? Rarely indeed is a person so full of spiritual maturity that he is completely detached from material goods. And how difficult it would be to find a single person whose soul was so married to poverty of life that he had no affection for any created thing. Such a person would be as rare as some oddity imported from the most distant land.

If a man gave away all his wealth, his act would merit him nothing. If he performed a severe penance, the merit would be but little. If he became the greatest scholar, he would be far from the goal. If his virtues were admirable and his devoutness was exemplary, he would still lack many things, especially the one necessary thing. And what is that necessary thing? It is this: to give up all one's attachments to things and persons (including oneself). Then, having done what he knows he should do to achieve such complete renouncing of his self-interest, he must think of it as but a small step, a sample of what true greatness would require. Let him think of himself as the unprofitable servant, as the Lord advises: "When you have done everything you have been commanded to do, say, 'We are useless servants' " (Luke 17.10). Then he will be truly poor and naked in spirit, and may join the prophet in saying, "I am alone and poor" (Psalm 24.16).

Yet no one would be wealthier than such a person. No one would be more powerful, no one more free. For he would have learned how to free himself from all things, and to consider himself the least of all.

xii. *Follow the royal road of the Cross.*
There are many who, hearing the words "Deny yourself, take up your cross, and follow me" (Matthew

16.24), find them hard. But it will be much harder to hear those other words: "Depart from me, you cursed, into everlasting fire" (Matthew 25.41). Those who accept the invitation to take up their cross need not fear they will hear themselves condemned on Judgment Day. The sign of the cross will appear in the heavens when the Lord comes as Judge. Then all the servants who embraced the cross, who united themselves in this life with the Crucified One, will approach Christ their Judge in hope and trust.

Why should you or anyone fear to take up the cross, when in that way one can win a kingdom? In the cross, we find salvation; in the cross, we find our life; in the cross, we have protection from our enemies; through the cross, we enjoy a foretaste of Heaven; through the cross, we gain strength of will; through the cross, we have spiritual joy; through the cross, our virtues are perfected; through the cross, perfect holiness can be ours. Apart from the cross, there is neither salvation for our souls nor hope of attaining everlasting life.

So take up your cross. Follow Jesus. In that way, you *will* enter eternal life. Jesus opened the way for you by carrying his cross and dying on it. He died for you, so that you too could take up your own cross and desire to die on it. If you die *with* Jesus and share in his sufferings, you will live with him. If you share his sufferings, you will share his glory.

Consider what this means: in the cross, we find everything; and everything depends on our dying upon it. There is no other way to eternal life; there is no other way to authentic peace of spirit. It is the way of the holy cross and daily penance. No matter where you go or where you look, you will not find a superior way, nor a more abject (but safer) way, than that of the holy cross. You can try to arrange your life so that everything is as you desire it; but you will find that you cannot eliminate suffering from your life, despite your efforts. Hence, you will always find the cross.

Either you will experience bodily pains, or you will know anguish in your soul. You will at times feel the pain of being forsaken by God; at times, those among whom you live will cause you pain. What is harder to bear is that you will often grow weary even of yourself. You cannot escape suffering; there is no simple remedy or salve you can apply to restore yourself to comfort; you must simply bear it as long as God wills it. What God desires is that you learn to bear your trials patiently, without looking for escape from them. He desires that you place your welfare in his hands and use your sufferings to teach you humility. No one can appreciate the passion of Christ better than one who suffers a similar trial.

Your cross always stands ready; it awaits you each day of your life. No matter where you go, you cannot escape it. No matter where you go, you must take yourself with you and will always have to bear up with yourself. No matter where you turn—up, down, outside, inside—you will find a cross everywhere, in everything. That is why you must cultivate the virtue of patience: only through patience will you know peace and win an eternal crown.

If you willingly take up your cross, you will find that it will lead you toward the goal you desire; there, indeed, you will suffer no more, but here, in this life, the cross involves suffering. If you take up your cross grudgingly, you increase its weight on your shoulders; it is a burden that only you can bear. If you should try to escape from one cross, you will only find yourself having to carry another—and perhaps a heavier one. In any case, how could you expect to avoid what no mortal man can avoid? Can you think of a saint whose life was free of trials? Not even our Lord Jesus Christ: every hour he lived on earth, he knew the pain of his passion. "It is written that the Messiah must suffer and rise again from the dead" and "thus enter into his glory" (Luke 24.46, 26). By what reasoning, then, do you look for another way than this—the royal road of the cross?

How can you wish to have a life of rest and enjoyment when you see that the whole life of Christ was a cross, a martyrdom? Do you not merely deceive yourself if you seek to escape suffering? Isn't this mortal life we have full of misery, and doesn't it present us crosses on all sides?

Understand, too, that the more spiritual progress a person makes, the heavier, often, will he find his crosses. The reason is that, as his love for God increases, the pain he feels in this place of exile also increases. Despite his many afflictions, he still remains hopeful of respite from them because he knows that the cross he carries will earn him his reward. By bearing his cross willingly, he finds that the pains his difficulties cause him increase his hope that God will comfort him. Furthermore, the more his body feels the discomfort, the more his soul is strengthened by an infusion of grace. It is not uncommon for someone to get such strength from willingly accepting his trials (accepting, that is, the cross of Christ) that he loses all desire to be free of them. He has reached the point of seeing that he will be more worthy in God's sight if he is able to endure even worse hardship without complaint as an act of love for God.

Of course, it is only by the grace of Christ that a person can become so fervent of spirit that he teaches his body to accept pain, which by nature it flees from.

To carry the cross . . . to love the cross . . . to do bodily penance . . . to bring the body to subjection . . . to flee honors . . . to accept the contempt of others without anger . . . to think little of ourselves and to wish others to do the same . . . to accept patiently any adversity or loss . . . to desire no prosperity in this life—these are not the ways of man. If you had only your own strength to draw on, you could follow none of them. It is only because you place your trust in the Lord that you have the strength—a strength from Heaven—to make the world and the flesh subject to your command. If you have the armor of faith and are signed with the cross of Christ, you have no reason to fear your enemy, the devil.

Your first step, then, is to be a good and faithful servant of Christ and bravely take up his cross, remembering that he was crucified for you. Prepare yourself to suffer many kinds of pain during this life of misery. Our lives are going to be troubled and even miserable, no matter where we are. Even if you were to try to hide from misery, it would find you. So it is, and so it must be. And because there is no way to escape the pains and sorrows of this life, we must bear them.

If you wish to be a friend of Jesus, drink from the chalice of his passion because you love him. As for spiritual consolation and blessing, let God do as he pleases on your behalf. Meanwhile, accept your pains and think of them as the best of consolations. Even if you had to undergo them without God's help, you would find that they are a small price to pay for the glory that awaits you.

When you reach the stage where your sufferings seem pleasant and welcome, because you accept them out of love for Christ, then will you be fortunate indeed. You will have found paradise on earth! But if you continue to look upon your sufferings as bothersome and try to escape them, you will only make yourself miserable; and the pains you try to escape from will dog your steps everywhere. If you give careful thought to the important things—your sufferings now, and eventually your death—you would soon draw yourself up to a better state of life and thus find the peace you are seeking.

Even if, like Saint Paul, you were to be taken up to the "third heaven," you would not be freed from suffering as a result. As the Lord said of Paul: "I myself will show him what he must suffer in my name" (Acts 9.16).

If you desire to love Jesus and to serve him for the remainder of this life, suffering will be your lot. How good it is to be worthy to suffer some pain in the name of Jesus! What glory it would bring you; what joy it would give the saints; and what encouragement it would give to those you live among! Everyone is ready to recommend patience; but few are willing to practice it. When you consider that some people are willing to suffer much for worldly goals, you have good reason to suffer a little for Christ.

Bring yourself to see that yours must be a "dying" sort of life. The more a person dies to himself (that is, gives up selfishness), the more he or she shares in God's life.

One who has not been willing to suffer hardship for Jesus' sake is hardly fit to share the joy of Heaven. To suffer willingly, out of love for Christ—nothing is more acceptable to God, nothing more to your advantage in this life. If you had the choice, you would do better to choose to suffer for Christ than to receive many blessings from him. Through suffering, you become more like him, and more like the saints. Pleasure and comfort win us no spiritual merit or growth; only sorrows and pain can do that, if we accept them willingly.

If there were a better way—one more likely to lead us to salvation—than suffering, Christ would have shown it to us in his word and example. But what he clearly told his disciples, and all others also who wish to be his followers, is this: "If anyone wishes to come after me, let him deny himself, take up his cross daily, and follow me" (Luke 9.23).

So after we have gathered all that has been written on the subject, this is the conclusion we are led to: it is through suffering much that we enter the kingdom of God.

Book Three

The Imitation of Christ

BOOK THREE

Spiritual Consolation

i. *Christ counsels the faithful soul.*

"I shall hear what the Lord God will speak to me" (Psalm 84.9). —Blessed is the soul who hears the Lord speaking within her, and is consoled by words from his own lips. Blessed also are the ears that can catch divine whisperings but ignore worldly murmurings. Blessed indeed are the ears that hear the inner truth, rather than only the voices of others. Blessed are the eyes that are not held entranced by external things but closely watch the things of the heart. Blessed are they who, by spiritual insight, use each day to improve their understanding of religious mysteries. Blessed are they who have decided to offer their hours to God and who keep themselves apart from the distractions of the world.

Think on these matters, my soul. Close the door to the senses, and then listen to what the Lord, your Beloved, says to you: "I am your salvation. I am your peace and your life. Stay with me, and you will have peace. Give no thought to passing things; seek after eternal things. Do you not see that transient goods will lead you away from me? And what good will anything created do you if you find yourself cut off from your Creator?" Leave aside all worldly vanities, then, and look for ways to make yourself pleasing and faithful to your Creator. In that way you will find a true happiness.

ii. *Truth speaks to us without the need for words.*

THE DISCIPLE:

"Speak, Lord, for your servant listens" (1 Kings 3.9). "I am your servant. Give me the understanding so that I may know your ordinances" (Psalm 118.125). "Bend my heart to observe your ordinances" (Isaiah 118.36). Let your word "drench me like the dew" (Deuteronomy 32.2).

The children of Israel once said to Moses: "Speak to us, and we shall listen to you; but do not let the Lord speak to us, or we shall die" (Exodus 20.19). O Lord, I do not pray in that way. Instead, like your prophet Samuel, I ask you, humbly and earnestly: "Speak, Lord, for your servant listens."

I do not desire that Moses or any of your other prophets speak to me. I desire that you, Lord God, who inspired and enlightened the prophets, speak to me. You have no need of them to instruct me perfectly; but they can do nothing for me without your assistance. Their words may be fine, but they cannot give me your

Spirit. They may be skilled orators, but they cannot set fire to my heart if you do not speak through them. They may give me your message, but you help me understand it. When they speak of mysteries, it is you who unlock their meaning for me. They tell me your commandments, but you help me live according to your will. They tell me the path I should follow; you give me the strength I need for the journey. Their advice comes to me from outside; you instruct and enlighten my heart. Their words are like water that soaks the ground; but you make the ground fruitful. Their words ring loudly in the air; but you give the gift of understanding to the hearer.

So I pray that, rather than Moses, you, O Lord my God, who are everlasting Truth, speak directly to me. If I have to depend only on the advice of others and am not enlivened by your Spirit, I may bear no fruit and thus die. I fear that the word I have heard but not kept, known but not loved, believed but not obeyed, may rise up to condemn me.

Therefore speak, Lord, for your servant listens. "You have the words of eternal life" (John 6.69). Speak and give comfort to my soul, so that I may amend my life for your praise, glory, and everlasting honor.

iii. *Listen humbly to the words of God, which many ignore.*
THE VOICE OF CHRIST:
My child, hear what I say to you. My words, most sweet to the ear, convey more knowledge than that of all the philosophers and scholars of earth. My words are spirit

and life. They cannot be weighed by human under-standing. They are not to be repeated as a show of learning, but heard in silence. They are to be heard humbly and given the heart's welcome.

THE DISCIPLE:

Then I said: "O Lord, happy is the one whom you ad-monish and teach the meaning of your law, so as to show him the way to peace during the days of evil" (Psalm 93.12); and thus to save him from feeling aban-doned on the earth.

THE VOICE OF CHRIST:

From the beginning, I was the teacher of the prophets. And still today, I speak to every human person. Many today are hard of heart; many, deaf to my voice, are more ready to hear what the world says than what God says. They are quick to follow their fleshly appetites, slow to seek after the pleasure of God. They busy them-selves doing the world's business, though the world can offer them only small and temporary rewards. When I promise great and eternal rewards, their hearts grow dull. Where are those who show as much interest in serving and obeying me as many show to the world and its masters?

"Be ashamed, O Sidon, for the sea has spoken" (Isaiah 23.4). And why? Because many will hardly lift a foot to move along the path to eternal life, and yet the same persons would willingly undertake an earthly voyage for some small advantage. They are hungry for any petty reward, and I sometimes see them going shame-lessly to courts of law to gain a pittance. They are ready to work day and night for a bit of money or even a dubious promise. When it comes to a chance for an unending reward, a lasting benefit, or unfading honor and glory, it must be said to their shame that they cannot endure the least fatigue. Does it not shame you, a lazy and complaining servant, that so many work harder to bring themselves to damnation than you do for eternal life? Or that they take more interest in their vanities than you do in the truth?

Sometimes, of course, the expectations of the worldly are disappointed. But my promises have never deceived; I have never sent away empty-handed anyone who trusted me. What I promise to give, I give. I will keep my word to anyone who holds fast to his love for me till death. All who are virtuous will have their reward from me; I look after all who are devoted to me.

Write my words in your heart. Meditate on them carefully. When temptation comes to you, you will find that you need my counsel.

Whenever you do not understand something written in a letter to you, you can have it explained when you visit its author. I prefer to visit my followers in two ways—in temptation, and in consolation. Each day, I "read" them those two lessons: one to call them from their evil habits, the other to encourage them in good habits. Those who hear my words and reject them build up condemnation for themselves on the last day.

—*A Prayer for the Grace of Devotion*

O Lord my God, you are the source of all my good. Who am I that I dare speak to you? I am your least worthy servant, a little worm; and my spiritual poverty is worse than I care to admit. But because I am nothing, have nothing, and can do nothing of myself, be mindful of me. You alone are all-good, all-just, and all-holy. You can do all things, give all things, and fill all things. Only the sinner do you leave empty-handed. Be merciful and fill my heart with your grace. I know that you do not wish your works to be in vain; yet how can I endure this life of misery unless you comfort me with your merciful grace? Do not hide your face from me. Do not put off your coming to my aid. Do not take your consolation from me; for otherwise you will see my soul become like a desert. Teach me to live according to your will, worthily and humbly. You are my wisdom. You know me truly. Even before the world was made and I was born into it, you knew me.

iv. *Walk humbly and honestly in God's sight.*

THE VOICE OF CHRIST:

My child, walk before me in truth. Seek after me with a simple heart. Anyone who lives in that way will be protected from the assaults of the evil one. My truth will save you from the seductions and lies of the wicked. If my truth has made you free, then you will indeed be free, and the words of others will not harm you.

THE DISCIPLE:

O Lord, you speak to me truly. May it be for me as you say. Let your truth be my teacher, and protect me till death. Let it free me from my evil tendencies and misplaced affections. And then I shall be able to walk with you, with a free heart.

THE VOICE OF CHRIST:

I shall teach you what is right and pleasing to my eyes. First, look upon your sins with deep pain and sorrow, and do not boast of your good works. You really are still a sinner, subject to many passions and often entangled in them. You are unable to be your own guardian. Quickly you stumble; quickly you are overcome; quickly you find yourself in trouble, and are undone. You have nothing you can pride yourself on; but you can find many reasons for thinking yourself a wretch. You are weaker than you imagine. So do not call "great" anything you do. For nothing is truly great or valuable or desirable that is not everlasting. Make eternal truth your chief pleasure; and then let your own unworthiness be your chief displeasure. Do not fear or shun or flee from anything till you have first feared, shunned, and fled from your sins and evil habits. Learn to be saddened by them more than you are by merely material losses.

There are some who walk before me but are not sincere. Their curiosity and pride lead them to wish to know my secrets and to become regarded as experts about the high things of God. They meanwhile are careless and neglect their own salvation. Because they lack my friendship, their pride and curiosity push them toward serious temptation and sins.

So this I say: fear the judgment of God; fear his anger. Instead of talking about the works of the Most

High, examine your own sinfulness. Teach yourself to see the ways in which you have offended the Lord, as well as the ways you have failed to do the good you could have done.

Some base their devotion entirely on books or pictures or other external things. Some have me on their lips but not in their hearts. Yet there are others whose understanding and affections have been enlightened and purified; they long for what is everlasting. Worldly affairs do not interest them; and only with reluctance do they do what nature requires for the maintenance of life. They have heard what the Spirit of Truth has spoken within their hearts. He has taught them to place no value in earthly goods and to love only the things of Heaven. Each day and each night, they lose some of their attachment to the world and desire more ardently the things of Heaven.

v. *Learn to love God as God loves you.*

THE DISCIPLE:

Heavenly Father, and Father of my Lord Jesus Christ, I bless you for having been mindful of your unworthy creature. I give you thanks, Father of mercies and God of spiritual comforting, for offering me comfort though I did not deserve it. I bless and glorify you, and your only-begotten Son, and the Holy Spirit, the Paraclete, forever and ever.

Dear Lord God, when you come into my heart, your holy love fills me with rejoicing. My heart finds all its happiness and joy in you. You are my hope and my refuge when sorrow encloses me. My love for you is still weak, and my virtues are not yet perfect; so I come to you for strength and comfort. Visit me often. Teach me your holy discipline. Free me from my evil habits. Cleanse my heart of its greed and envy. When you have healed and purified my soul, I shall be firm in perseverance, strong in time of suffering, and skilled in the ways of love.

Love is a great and wonderful blessing. It makes every difficulty easy, and it bears all wrongs calmly. It carries burdens without feeling their weight; it makes bitter things seem sweet. The noble love I have for Jesus moves me to deeds of charity and makes me wish to become perfect. That love lifts me up; it is not limited by anything ignoble. It works to free me from worldliness of life, keeps my vision clear, and helps me through adversity.

Compared to love, nothing is sweeter, stronger, higher, or wider; nothing is more pleasant, nothing more ample. Neither in Heaven nor on earth is there anything superior to a love that is born of God and yearns for God, who is above all created things.

Such love makes us fly, run, and rejoice; it makes us free, so that nothing can enslave us. It makes us want to give all for all and to possess all in all. That is because it has its source in the single greatest Good, who is above all things. From him flows and comes every other good. Those who love him look beyond all his gifts to the Giver.

Love sometimes seems to have no limits; it overflows all bounds. It feels no burdens, is undisturbed by troubles, strives for more than it can accomplish, and does not know the word "impossible." It thinks it may and can do all things; and in fact it often succeeds and brings about many good results when others, not motivated by love, fail at similar attempts.

Love is also watchful. When we sleep, it remains awake. In our weariness, it does not tire. When we are alarmed, it remains calm. Like a dancing flame of a torch, it moves upward despite all obstacles and passes through them unharmed.

If a person loves, he will know the sound of love's voice. Love is a warm affection of soul; it is like a voice calling to the ears of God, saying: "My God, my love, I belong entirely to you, and you to me. Give me an increase of love; I wish to taste with my heart the sweetness of love; I wish to be submerged in your love and to bathe in it. Let me be captured by love; let it lift me above myself into a state of fervor and wonder. Let me sing the hymn of love, while following you, my Love, to the highest heaven. Let my soul exhaust itself in praising you joyfully and lovingly. Let me love you more than I love myself; and let me love myself only because you love me. Let me love all others who love you, as I am commanded by your law of love (which shines forth from you)."

Love is swift, kind, pleasant, and a delight. It is strong, patient, faithful, prudent, long-suffering, and brave. It is never selfish (for if ever a person seeks his own self-interest, he fails in love). Love is circumspect, humble, and conscientious. It is not something soft or frivolous; it is not at all concerned about worldly things.

Love is temperate and chaste, steadfast and quiet, and stands guard over the senses. It recommends us to religious obedience. It never looks upon itself with pride, but is turned to God in thankful devotion. It trusts and hopes in him, even through those times when he temporarily loses his attractiveness to us (for even those who love God must pass through times of sorrow).

Then too, a person who is unwilling to accept the sufferings that come his way and resign himself to what God asks of him is not properly called a friend of God. A lover willingly takes on difficulties for the sake of the beloved, and does not abandon the beloved when difficulties appear.

vi. *A lover must pass several tests of fidelity.*

THE VOICE OF CHRIST:

My child, you are not yet a brave or wise lover.

THE DISCIPLE:

Lord, tell me why.

THE VOICE OF CHRIST:

When you meet the smallest obstacle, you abandon your efforts; and you are too quick to find some comfort for yourself.

If you were a steadfast lover, you would stand firm against temptations and be untroubled by the sly arguments of your enemy the devil. In good times, you would find me pleasing; but the same would be true in bad times. If you were a wise lover, you would place less value on my gifts and more value on the love that leads me to give them. The wise lover is more inter-

ested in the affection of the beloved than in any gift
the beloved might give; for the beloved is more valued
than any gift. One who loves me with a noble love
knows that I am myself more worthy of love than any
gift could make me.

Yet you must not lose hope if you sometimes feel a
spiritual dryness or lack of devotion toward me and my
saints. The pleasant feeling that you sometimes experience in your soul is caused by my grace; it is a foretaste
of the joy of Heaven, your true home. It is a feeling that
comes and goes; so do not become addicted to it. Your
struggle against evil thoughts that arise within you
shows your good virtue and gains you merit. Do not let
your imagination cause you any upset, no matter what
images it shows you. Hold tightly to your spiritual
promises, and keep an honest relationship with God.

This spiritual ecstasy or rapture you sometimes experience is no fantasy of your own; nor is the sudden
lapse into your ordinary state of weakness. The latter
state is an evil you must endure (not one you commit);
and so long as you resist your own weakness, you will
be making spiritual progress.

Obviously the Ancient Enemy—the devil—uses
every means in his power to turn your will from what
is good and cause you to find devotional practices distasteful. He will especially try to turn you away from
venerating the saints, from meditating on my Passion,
and from desiring to grow in virtue. By filling your
mind with evil thoughts, he hopes to wear you down
and disturb your life, so that you will be less inclined

toward prayer and spiritual reading. He counts it as a loss to himself whenever you confess your sins humbly; and if he could find a way, he would discourage your receiving Holy Communion.

Do not put any faith in him; do not even pay any attention to him. He is skilled at setting deceitful traps. Whenever he presents you with some invitation to evil, challenge him, saying, "Get you gone, filthy demon! Heap shame on yourself, miserable wretch! You are vile to whisper such things in my ears. Away with you, hateful temptor. You will get no cooperation from me, for Jesus is my strength; your efforts are in vain. I would rather die and suffer every torment you can cause me than fall in league with you. Be silent, and depart from me. I shall have nothing to do with you; you cause me nothing but trouble. 'The Lord is my light and my salvation. Whom should I fear?' [Psalm 27.1]. Even if entire armies threatened my life, I would not fear. The Lord is my helper and my redeemer."

If you fight like a good soldier, even if you sometimes fall from weakness, you will be able to rise again, stronger than ever, trusting in the help of my grace. Presumption and a foolish underestimation of the enemy are what you must watch out for. Many fall into sin because of such attitudes, and sometimes become almost completely blind to their danger. Let the example of those who are undone by their own self-satisfaction be your warning, and encourage in you a proper humility.

vii. *Make humble use of the gift of grace.*

THE VOICE OF CHRIST:

When you receive the grace of devotion, do not congratulate yourself about it or even think or speak much of it. It is better—safer—for you to hide the fact, to look upon it in all humility, wondering whether you are even worthy of it. If you rely too much on it, you could cancel it. Instead, when grace is with you, think about how weak and lacking you are without it. Making spiritual progress is not the same thing as enjoying graces of consolation. To make progress, you must teach yourself to accept their withdrawal humbly, patiently, and without complaint. Do not use the lack of such grace as an excuse for becoming lax in your prayers or neglecting your other duties. No, you must go on and do what you can, as well as you can; you must not lose interest in your spiritual welfare during a period of dryness and anxiety.

As you know, many people quickly lose all patience and self-discipline when their lives do not prosper. It is not within the power of any human being to plan the future in every detail. It is God's prerogative to offer his grace as he wishes, in the amount he wishes, to whomever he wishes, according to his pleasure.

Some presumptuous persons, relying too much on the grace of devotion, have pushed themselves into disaster because they tried to do what was beyond their strength. They ignored the evidence of their own weakness, and let themselves be led by their emotions rather than by their good judgment. And precisely because they took upon themselves to go beyond what would please God, they lost the grace he had given them. They had all but built themselves homes in Heaven, only to find themselves helpless, spiritual outcasts, embarrassed and empty-handed. They still had to learn that they could not fly with their own wings, but needed to trust in mine.

Those who are still inexperienced in the ways of the Lord are easily fooled, and soon undone, unless they are guided by wiser persons. If they prefer their own counsel to that of others with more spiritual experience, they put themselves in jeopardy of coming to a sad end—especially if they resist the warnings that call them from their pride.

How seldom do those with an inflated opinion of themselves show a willingness to accept the guidance of others. Yet it is much better to seek a little wisdom with an attitude of docility than to work at becoming learned with an attitude of stubborn self-sufficiency. As a rule, it is better for you to have little than to have much; the latter only leads to pride.

Then too, someone who devotes his life to pleasure is hardly wise. Such a one forgets his helplessness and vulnerability; not being chastened by any fear of the Lord, he cares not whether he might reject a grace when it is offered him. Foolish too is one who, in a time of sorrow or trouble, gives up all hope and becomes despondent; such a one does not place a proper confidence in me. On the other hand, it is not good to become complacent during a time of peace; for then you will only be more likely to panic and give up when you are put to a trial.

If you had the wisdom to keep your outlook humble (and thus see your own smallness), and if you governed your spiritual life as you should, you would be in little danger of causing any harm to yourself.

When you feel the fire of devotion kindled within you, what you should think about is how you will live when the flame of it dies. When it does die, remember that it is I who have taken it away for a time as a warning to you, and that it may return again as a sign of my glory. A period of trial can often do you more good than having your life unfold as you would prefer.

A person's merits are measured not by heavenly visions or graces, but by knowledge of the Scriptures; not by rising to a position of seniority to others, but by the sincerity of his humility, by the extent of his God-like charity, and by his unrelenting effort to seek only and fully the honor of God. It is good to admit honestly your own lowliness; it is even better to have others spurn and humiliate you than to have them look up to you.

viii. *Ask God to show you what you truly are.*

THE DISCIPLE:

I, who am dust and ashes, will speak to you, Lord. If I consider myself anything more than that, you stand ready to correct me; and my sins bear witness to the truth about myself, which I cannot deny. If I look down on myself and see my nothingness, and if I avoid all self-congratulation and think of myself as the dust of which I am made, I will know the consolation of your grace, and your light will fill my heart.

All my pride will drown in the depths of my nothingness. There you show me to myself. You show me what I am, what I have been, and what I am becoming. I am nothing but did not know it. Of myself, I am totally without strength. But if you but look upon me for an instant, I am immediately strong and filled anew with joy. Of my own weight, I sink to the depths; yet how quickly you lift me up and embrace me with your grace. It is your love that has this effect on me, holding me up, supporting me through so much I have to undergo, protecting me from many mortal dangers, and snatching me—I hardly exaggerate—from countless evils. By loving myself too much, I lost sight of my real self. By seeking and loving you alone, I found both myself and you. And that same love has shown me how, at bottow, I really am as nothing. Yet you care for me far beyond whatever I deserve, far beyond what I dare hope or ask for.

So I bless you, my God. Unworthy as I am of your gifts to me, you, in your majesty and goodness, seek constantly to share your benefits even with those who are far from you and who show you no gratitude. Draw all hearts to yourself, so that they may become humble, devout, and thankful. You are our salvation, our courage, and our strength.

ix. *Look upon all creation as coming from, and belonging to, God.*

THE VOICE OF CHRIST:

My child, if you desire to become holy, look to me as the goal of your life. If you live with that goal always in mind, your passions, which so often lead to selfishness and to sinful attachment to material things, will be guarded. The minute you seek your own advantage in earthly affairs, your interior life will begin to die, and your heart will dry up.

Look upon all created things in their relation to me, for I have made them what they are. Recall that all material goods have their origin in the one perfect Good, and therefore belong to me; I am their source, and to their source all things must one day return.

The poor and the rich, the lowly and the mighty, all have their life from me, the flowing Fountain of Life. And those who acknowledge their dependence on me and freely offer me their service will receive grace upon grace from me. But the person who grasps after possession of things without consideration for me, or who acts as if some created good belonged solely to him, will experience neither joy nor happiness in his heart. The greedy person in many ways causes himself to carry a heavy burden of distress. In your own case, then, do not give yourself the credit for any good you do, nor give another full credit for any virtue, but turn thankfully to God, without whom no human being has anything at all!

I am the giver of all that exists. It is my will that all things be returned again to me, and I particularly look for the thanks that is due me. So you see, to recognize this truth is to put all vainglorious thoughts to flight.

The human heart *inspired by heavenly grace and divine charity* knows neither envy nor greed nor pride. My love overcomes all weaknesses; it strengthens the powers of the soul. It is the best wisdom to find your joy in me alone. For only God is wholly good. He is to be praised above all else; in all things, offer him your blessing.

x. *To serve God rather than the world is the surest way to know joy.*

THE DISCIPLE:

Lord, now I shall speak again and not hold myself silent. I shall say to my Lord God, the King of Heaven: "How many, O Lord, are the signs of your goodness, which you have prepared for those who love you!" (Psalm 31.19). How do those who love you and serve you with their whole heart look upon you?

Certainly, words cannot describe the sweetness of contemplating you—a gift you give those who love you. You have shown me the sweetness of your own love, above all by having brought me into existence, also by calling me back to your service when I had strayed from it, and even by commanding me to love you. O everflowing Fountain of Love, what shall I say to you? How can I ever forget you when you did not forget me after I died through sin? You have shown me more mercy than I could hope for, and have offered me your grace and friendship when I did not deserve them.

How can I repay you for your blessings? It is not the

calling of every person on earth to give up all possessions, abandon the things of the world, and adopt a religious life. In what way am I a better person if I serve you, you whom all are obliged to serve? I can take no pride in my calling; I should instead be honored that you would accept me into your service, for I am unworthy of it and have little to offer in it. Even the very things with which I might serve you belong to you. You created the earth and the heavens for man; and each day they stand ready to do as you command. More than that, you created the angels to minister to us. And most amazing of all, you have placed yourself at our service and have promised to give yourself to us.

How can I repay you for the untold thousands of blessings you have extended to all of human estate? I wish that I could serve you worthily all my life—or even one day! I know that you are worthy of all my service, of all honor, and of unending praise. You are, in truth, my Lord; and I, your poor servant, am bound to devote myself to doing your will, to praising you without slacking. This is my wish, my desire. I ask you to perform through me whatever I cannot perform of myself.

Let me find it an honor and a glory to serve you, and to detach myself from created goods for your sake. I know that those who willingly place themselves in your service will have the reward of your gracious assistance. Those who deny themselves all bodily pleasures as a sign of their love for you will experience the consolations of the Holy Spirit. Those who walk the narrow path and keep apart from worldly cares in honor of your holy name will be rewarded with peace of mind.

The service of God is sweet and joyful; it makes us truly free and holy. This bondage to religious life is holy; it makes a person equal to the angels, pleasing to God, a terror to demons, and deserving of the encouragement of all believers. It is a way of service to be embraced strongly and held to in faith; the reward it offers is the highest Good, and the joy that it wins is everlasting.

xi. *Place some limits on the desires of your heart.*

THE VOICE OF CHRIST:

My child, you have not yet mastered many things you must learn well.

THE DISCIPLE:

What are they, Lord?

THE VOICE OF CHRIST:

First, you need to desire for yourself only what I desire for you. Do not be so concerned to love yourself properly, as to do what I ask of you. Very often you will find yourself moved along and even inflamed by your desires; and you should then stop and consider whether they arise from your intention to do me honor or to bring *you* some worldly advantage. If your desires arise from your love for me, you will be content with whatever my providence desires for you. But if your motives are in any way self-seeking, you will find yourself unsatisfied and depressed. So be watchful. Do not allow yourself to be caught up by some desire of your own cultivation without any thought of me; later, you will only regret your poor judgment and find no pleasure in something that seemed to promise it. You must learn that what seems good is not immediately to be sought after; nor should you be too quick to reject everything that seems distasteful.

Sometimes you do well to treat even your nobler desires and inclinations with restraint. Too much enthusiasm can blind you to what is reasonable; it can lead you into scandalous behavior; and it can bring you to a sudden fall and discouragement if you find others resisting you.

Sometimes, too, you must resist your own bodily appetites vigorously, even violently. Pay no attention to what the flesh does or does not desire. Instead, take steps to see that you keep your body's appetites under the control of your soul, using force if necessary. The body needs to be disciplined and kept in its proper place. You must teach it to be prepared for anything, to be satisfied with little, to find its pleasure in simple things, and not to complain about petty annoyances.

xii. *Learn patience in acquiring control of your bodily appetites.*

THE DISCIPLE:

I see, O Lord God, that I must be patient in dealing with the many trials and frustrations of this life. I see that my life can never be entirely free of sadness or trials, no matter how I might try to ensure its peace.

THE VOICE OF CHRIST:

There is truth in your words, my child; but remember that I do not wish you to seek a peace that leaves you free of temptations or the opposition of others. I would much prefer that you consider yourself as having found peace when your life is most beset by trials and hardships.

If you protest that you cannot bear much suffering, how will you endure the purgatorial flames? Of two evils, the lesser is always preferable. It is better, therefore, to bear patiently the evils of this life, out of love for God, so that you can escape an everlasting punishment.

Do you think that those other, worldly persons live with little or no suffering? Ask even those who live surrounded by material goods, and they will tell you a different story. You may say, "Yes, but they do not feel burdened by their troubles because they can live as they please and are comforted by many pleasures." To be sure, they seem to have whatever they desire—but how long will they have it? Take note: in this world, the prosperous disappear like smoke, and no one remembers their earlier joys. Even in this life, the comfort they derive from their pleasures is always mixed with bitterness, fear, and melancholy. The very things that bring them pleasure often bring them a penalty or sorrow too. You can see the justice of this: they place no restraints of reason on their search for pleasures, so they cannot enjoy them without feelings of shame and regret.

In their drunk-like blindness, people do not understand how fleeting, how misleading, how inhuman, and how shameful it is to seek only the pleasures of the flesh. They willingly suffer the deaths of their souls in order that, like brutish animals, they may pursue the low enjoyments of a degenerate life.

You can see, my child, why I advise you not to be a slave to your own will and lusts. "Take delight in the Lord, and he will give you whatever your heart desires" (Psalm 37.4). If you wish to experience the blessing of true delight and be strongly comforted by me, ample consolations will be given you *if* you separate yourself from worldly things and low pleasures. The farther you withdraw yourself from any dependence on the consolations of others, the fuller and sweeter will be the comforts I send you.

At first, you will win these blessings only through the pain of hard work and struggle. Your present habits of life will resist your efforts, but eventually you will acquire a better habit. Your body will put up a struggle, but your spirit will tame and harness it. The Ancient Serpent will test and torment you, but your prayers will put him to flight. Through your constancy and your useful work, you will place a barrier between him and you.

xiii. *True obedience is to live after the example of Jesus.*
THE VOICE OF CHRIST:
My child, anyone who tries to avoid showing me obedience only succeeds in withdrawing from my grace. In the same way, one who seeks only his personal advantage loses those privileges which belong to all. The monk or friar who does not willingly and freely submit himself to his religious superior gives evidence

that his flesh is not fully under the control of his soul but still fights and murmurs against him.

If you wish to conquer your own flesh, make it your first goal to submit yourself to your own religious superior. If your soul is not exhausted from sparring with the flesh, she will be better able to resist the outer Enemy. If your body does not live in harmony with your soul, you are your own worst enemy and the source of most trouble to yourself. You absolutely must learn to view your own selfishness with contempt if you hope ever to be victorious over your own flesh and blood.

It is because you still love yourself too much that you hesitate to place yourself wholly under the will of others. Why should you think it such a great loss to subject yourself to others of human estate—you who are but dust and nothing—when you see that I, the all-powerful Most High who created all things out of nothing, humbly made myself subject to other men, for your sake? I made myself the humblest and the least of men so that you might learn from my humility to overcome your selfishness and pride.

You who are but dust: learn to obey. You who are but earth and clay: learn to humble yourself. Bow yourself down under the foot of *every* person. Learn to break your own willfulness; submit yourself to all in authority over you. Take arms with zeal against yourself. Let no trace of pride be sheltered within you. Make yourself into one so humble and lowly that all may "trample over" you as if you were dust in the street.

What is there that you, in your vanity, can properly

complain of? When others complain about you, how can you, a weak sinner who has so many times offended God and merited Hell, defend yourself? I have looked on you with a merciful eye because your soul is precious to me. I have desired that you might know of my love for you, and that you would devote your life to humble subjection of yourself and patient endurance of the contempt others have for you.

xiv. *Learn to judge yourself as God judges you.*
THE DISCIPLE:
Lord, your judgments thunder around me and shake my bones. My soul trembles in fear. I am overcome with awe when I think that even the starry heavens are blemished in your sight; that you found wickedness among the angels and did not spare those who embraced it. What, then, will happen to me? Stars have fallen from the skies; so how can I, who am but dust, be presumptuous? Many whose deeds were once praised have fallen to the depths of Hell. Even I have seen some who, having once eaten the Bread of Angels, gave themselves to gluttonous feeding on the husks of swine.

Lord, if you withdraw your hand, there is no grace. If you cease to guide us, we have no wisdom. If you no longer defend us, we have no courage. If you do not strengthen it, our chastity is vulnerable. If you do not keep a holy watch over us, our watchfulness cannot protect us. By ourselves, we sink, we perish; when you are with us, we are uplifted, we live. We are shaky; you make us firm. We are lukewarm; you inflame us.

How humbly should I look upon myself! How little

I should value anything that seems praiseworthy in me! How fully I should place myself under your judgment, O Lord! For there indeed I find myself to be as nothing.

What an unbearable burden, what a boundless sea to find myself to be nothing but nothingness! How then can any self-glory hide in me? How can I possibly place any trust in my own virtue? O Lord, your judgments are like a deluge that swallows up all my selfishness.

What is this flesh, in your eyes? How can this clay claim any glory of its own against you, who formed it? How can anyone whose heart is fully obedient to God be "lifted up" by self-centeredness? Nothing in the whole world can be a source of pride for one whom Truth has subjected to himself. The one whose hopes are entirely placed in God will not be swayed by the tongues of flatterers. For those who flatter are themselves nothing; like the sounds of their words, they will all pass away. Only "the truth of the Lord remains forever" (Psalm 117.2).

xv. *In all things, seek the will of God.*

THE VOICE OF CHRIST:

My child, at every turn in your life, this is how you should call upon me: *Lord, if this is something pleasing to you, so be it. If it gives you honor, Lord, I do it in your name. If you judge it to be desirable and profitable to me, then grant that I may employ it for the glory of your name. But if you know that it will bring me harm and provide no benefit for my soul's welfare, then take from me all desire for it.*

Not every desire is prompted by the Holy Spirit, no

matter how "good" and "right" it may appear to be for you. It is difficult for you to know whether you are prompted by a good or evil spirit, or even whether it is your own selfishness that moves you. Many a person has been deceived by mistaking an evil spirit for a good one.

Whenever you see something you consider good for you to pursue, pray for it with humility of heart and renew your fear of God. Do not act until you have placed the matter before me in humble resignation, saying: *Lord, you know what is best for me. Let this or something else be granted me, as you judge best for me. Grant me whatever you know will be best for me, whatever will most please you, and whatever will best reveal your glory. Do with me as you prefer, in all things. In your hands, you hold me. Turn me in the direction you would send me. Look upon me as your servant, ready to obey you in all things. I desire to live for you, not for myself. And my one hope is that I may do so without fault or failure.*

—*A Prayer of Dedication to God's Will*

Most merciful Jesus, grant me your grace. May it remain with me, and sustain me, till my life's end. May I always desire and do only what you approve and find pleasing. May your will be my will. May my will follow the example of yours and agree perfectly with it. May my will be at one with yours in willing and not willing, so that I never act against your will.

Grant also that I may die to all worldly things and prefer to be despised and unknown in this life, because of my love for you. May it be my highest desire to rest in you, and find peace of heart in you. You alone are the heart's peace. You alone are its rest. Apart from you, every life is difficult and tormented. In your peace, most high and everlasting Good, I shall sleep and take my rest. Amen.

xvi. *The comfort we seek comes from God alone.*

THE DISCIPLE:

I do not look for anything in this life to provide the comfort I desire. I know I must look to the life hereafter for such comfort. If I should somehow enjoy every comfort and delight this world has to offer, I know they could not last. I have come to see that my soul will know complete consolation and delight only in God. He is the consoler of the poor, the helper of the humble.

Wait a while, my soul, wait for the divine promise to be fulfilled. In Heaven, you will be satisfied by all good things. If you look for too much consolation from this world's goods, you will lose your chance for the lasting goods of Heaven. The things of this world are for your use; but the things of Heaven are what you should desire. Worldly goods will not really satisfy you; you were not created simply so that you could enjoy them.

Possession of all created things would not satisfy you, my soul. Your entire happiness lies in God, who made all those things. The happiness that you and the other good and faithful servants of Christ await is not the same as that happiness which the worldly sort of person seeks and praises. In this life, those who are pure of heart and who live as citizens of Heaven sometimes enjoy a foretaste of Heaven's joy.

All merely human consolation is short-lived and of small value. But that consolation which we receive from the Truth is both true and blessed.

Devout persons take with them a consoler—Jesus—wherever they go. They say to him: *Be with me, Lord Jesus, at all times, in every place. Let it be the source of most comfort to have no desire for human comforting. If you should withdraw your comfort from me, I shall consider your will and your just testing of me to be my comfort. For I know that your anger will pass, and that you will not test me forever.*

xvii. *Entrust all your cares to God.*

THE VOICE OF CHRIST:

My child, allow me to shape your life according to my will. What is best for you, I best know. Your judgment is weak; your feelings are subject to the sway of your affections.

THE DISCIPLE:

Lord, you tell me what is true. You are more anxious for my welfare than I am for myself. Anyone who does not place all his anxieties on you will soon stumble under their weight. Lord, I desire only that my will remain committed to you, and that you should guide me as it pleases you. Whatever you lead me to must be good.

If it be your will that I live in darkness, blessed be your name. Or if it be your will that I live in the light, again shall I bless you. If you stoop down to offer me your comfort, I shall praise you. And if you should then have me put to a trial, still I shall praise you forever.

THE VOICE OF CHRIST:

My child, that is what your spiritual attitudes must be if you would walk beside me. You need to be as ready to suffer as to be happy. You ought to be as cheerful when poor and destitute as you would be if you were rich and lacked for nothing.

THE DISCIPLE:

Lord, for your sake, I shall cheerfully suffer whatever happens to me, as coming with your permission. I am prepared to accept from your hand both good fortune and bad, the sweet and the bitter, the joyful and the sorrowful. I shall be grateful for whatever happens to me. If you keep me safe from sin, I shall fear neither death nor Hell. So long as you do not cast me away from you forever or blot me from the Book of Life, I shall not be harmed by any distress or suffering.

xviii. *Let Christ be your model for bearing sufferings patiently.*

THE VOICE OF CHRIST:

My child, I came from Heaven to win your salvation. I took your miseries upon myself—not because I had to, but because I loved you. I desired that you might thus learn how to be patient and to bear your sufferings without complaint. For from the hour of my birth till my death on the cross, I was not without suffering and grief.

I suffered from the lack of earthly goods; I often heard many complain about me; I endured disgrace and calumnies without looking for revenge; my assistance often met with ingratitude; the miracles I performed were greeted with blasphemies; and my teachings about Heaven were opposed by the learned.

THE DISCIPLE:

Lord, your patience while you were on earth fulfilling the will of the Father teaches me that I also, who am but a miserable sinner, should live in patience, accepting your will for me. For as long as you desire, I shall bear the burdens of this mortal life, for the good of my soul. Though this present life often seems a heavy burden, I can make it a source of merit, with the help of your grace. Your own example and that of your saints have helped me to see this life as a brighter and more blessed time.

This life today brings us more consolations than was the case under the Old Law, when the gates of Heaven were closed, when the way to Heaven was hidden in darkness, and when so few were searching for the Eternal Kingdom. Before your sufferings and death had "paid the debt," those who were just and who merited salvation could not enter Heaven.

How many thanks I am bound to offer you, Lord, because you agreed to show me and all your faithful servants the good and right way to reach your everlasting kingdom. Your life is our way; it is with your patience that we walk more closely with you, our Crown. If you had not gone before us and shown us the way, who would have cared to follow it? Except for your holy example, many indeed would have remained far distant from you.

Even those of us who know of your miracles and teachings remain lukewarm. What would become of us if we had not so clear a light by which to follow you?

xix. *Prepare yourself to bear future sufferings after the example of Christ.*

THE VOICE OF CHRIST:

My child, in all of your meditations, think of my sufferings and those of the saints; then you will be less inclined to complain. After all, you have not yet had to suffer the shedding of your own blood. What you may suffer is but minor compared to the terrible things experienced by the saints. In many ways, they were sorely tempted, troubled, tried, and tormented. Be mindful therefore of the heavy woes of others, and you will be better able to bear the little ones that afflict you.

If your own troubles do not seem small to you, examine your conscience to see whether your own impatience is not making them seem worse than they are. Be they harsh or mild, try to bear all your trials patiently.

The better you prepare yourself to suffer patiently, the more wisely you will live, and the greater will be your reward. You will suffer more "easily" if you train your mind and habits of life properly.

Do not say, "I cannot bear to suffer this thing from

that person, nor is it right that I allow him to get away with such behavior; he has harmed my good name and accused me of doing things I have never even thought of doing! From someone else, perhaps, I will put up with as much ignominy as I may decide I deserve. . . . "

How foolish is such talk. It does not place any value on the virtue of patience or on the One who has promised to reward it. It considers only the person and the "offense" committed. The person who will suffer only as much as seems good, or who will accept suffering only from those who are "acceptable" sources of it, cannot be called patient.

A truly patient person does not stop to consider from whom the suffering comes—from an equal, a superior, or an inferior, from a holy or a perverse person. No matter how terrible a calamity befalls him, he accepts it gratefully—as if it came from the hand of God. And he considers it a benefit, because he knows that anything suffered for God's sake—no matter how small it be—earns him a reward.

Be prepared, therefore, for the fight, if you wish to be victorious. You cannot earn the crown of patience without a struggle. To refuse to suffer is to refuse the crown. But if you desire this crown, fight valiantly and bear up patiently. Just as without labor there can be no rest, so too without doing battle with yourself, no victory.

THE DISCIPLE:

O Lord, may that which seems by nature impossible to me become possible with the help of your grace. You already know how little I can endure my sufferings, how quickly I am discouraged by the slightest obstacle. May I find that every trial willingly accepted for your name's sake seems pleasant and welcome to me; for I believe that to accept sorrow and trouble for your sake is good for the life of my soul.

xx. *Let the sources of your discomforts teach you your weaknesses.*

THE DISCIPLE:

Before you, Lord, I shall testify against my own claim to righteousness and admit my weaknesses. So often it is but a little thing that throws me into a mood of sadness or disappointment. I *intend* to be brave, but even a slight temptation puts me in peril. Sometimes too, a little thing will be the beginning of a severe temptation. Just when I think I am safe and suspect no danger, a slight breeze often nearly topples my resolve.

Look on my weakness and lowliness, Lord, which you know so well, and have mercy on me. Rescue me from the quicksand that has caught hold of me, or I shall be without hope. It shames me to know that you know how ready I am to fall, how weak I am in resisting my own passions. While I try to resist my appetites, their assaults on me trouble and grieve me; and to live each day in this continuous struggle wearies me exceedingly.

Hateful thoughts come to me much more readily than they depart; and in this fact I measure my weakness. O most mighty God of Israel, lover of faithful souls, if only you would take into account the efforts and the sorrows of your servant and come to his assistance in every undertaking! Give me the strength of heavenly courage, so that the outer man, this misery-prone flesh, will not take command of me. I am obliged to continue my struggle against him so long as I draw breath in this life; for he is not yet under the firm control of the spirit.

Alas, what sort of life is this, never free of troubles and miseries, with traps and enemies on all sides! When one trouble passes or one temptation fades, another comes to replace it. Even while one source of conflict makes its assault, lo, many others launch their surprise attacks. How is it possible to love this life, with its terrible bitterness, when one is prey to so many different calamities and miseries? How, indeed, can it be called life—when so many forms of death and plague thrive on it? And yet, there are many who do love it and seek their happiness in it!

This world is often said to be deceitful and of no value; and yet it is not easy for us to part with it, because the appetites of the body hold sway over us. There are some things that encourage us to love this world, while others make us despise it. The lusts of the flesh, the lusts of the eyes, and the "pride of life" (1 John 2.16) encourage in us that attachment to the world; but the pains and miseries that are the consequences of pursuing our lusts awaken in us a weariness and a hatred of this same world.

The soul of one who is addicted to this world is soon overcome with a desire for vicious pleasures. She imagines that there are delights beyond the thorns, because she has never detected or tasted the sweetness of God, nor the delight that virtue brings. On the other hand, those who hold the world in proper contempt and who desire to live only for God, under the discipline of his holy law, have firsthand knowledge of the divine sweetness promised those who rightly renounce the world. These latter see very clearly how far the world is from the truth and in how many ways it deceives us.

xxi. *Look to God, rather than to created goods, for your comfort.*

THE DISCIPLE:

My soul, above and in all things, find your rest in God always; for he is the comforter of all the saints.

O most sweet and loving Jesus, grant me this blessing: that I may find my repose in you, who are above all created things, above all health and beauty, above all honor and glory, above every power and title, above all knowledge and intelligence, above all praise and renown, above all earthly sweetness and comfort, above my every hope and longing, and above what I deserve or desire. For you are above all the gifts and favors you can give us, and above the joy and happiness that our minds can receive or feel. Yea, you are above the angels, archangels, and the entire heavenly host, all things visible and invisible, and everything that is not you, my Lord and God.

Only you, O Lord, are supremely good, beyond every other good; you alone are the Most High, the Most Powerful; and your fullness and self-sufficiency are perfect. You alone are most sweet, most consoling, most lovable and loving, most noble and glorious, beyond all compare. All that is truly good is found perfectly in you; so it has always been, and so it will always be.

As long as I do not behold you and have not fully attained you, anything you might give me besides your very Self must seem less than I desire, and unsatisfying. For truly my heart cannot rest, or be fully content, till it rests in you, and thus rise above all other gifts and all created goods.

Would that I had the wings of true liberty, so that I might fly above this life and rest beside you, Lord of creation, spouse of my soul, purest lover, Jesus Christ! Alas, when shall I receive the gift of fully appreciating and seeing, in peace of mind, your incomparable sweetness? When shall I so love you that I forget myself and feel only your presence with all my senses beyond measure, and thus be gathered entirely up to you—in a union that I can only speak of and not describe?

But as it is, I now must endure my grief-born unhappiness amidst many sighs. For in this vale of tears there are many evils, which disturb, grieve, and overshadow my life. They oppose and distract me, seduce and trip me; they keep me from coming freely unto you and enjoying the warm welcoming with which you greet the spirits of the blessed. I pray that my present unhappiness and my pleas for relief may waken your compassion for me.

O Jesus, you who are the brightness of eternal glory and the comforter of the pilgrim soul, though my tongue cannot find its voice, listen to the silence I speak unto you.

How long does my Lord delay his coming? Let him come to me, his poor, despised servant, and bring me gladness. If he will but stretch out his hand, he can deliver a wretch from every anguish.

Come, Lord, come, for apart from you I have neither a joyful day nor a joyful hour. You alone are my joy. Without you, my table is empty.

I am but a wretched creature, and live as if imprisoned and weighted down with fetters—till you refresh me with the light of your presence, restore me to liberty, and show me your friendly countenance. Others may seek what they please rather than seek you; but I have no other source of delight, my God, except you alone. You are my hope and my everlasting salvation.

I shall not rest or cease to pray till your grace has returned to me, and I hear you speaking inwardly to me.

THE VOICE OF CHRIST:

Behold, here I am. Look up and see that I have come to you because you called out to me. The longing of your soul, along with your tears, humility, and sorrow for your sins, has won my interest and brought me to you.

THE DISCIPLE:

Lord, I have called to you, desiring to know your joy, and prepared to set aside all else for your sake. You have stirred up my heart to seek for you. Blessed are you, O Lord, for showing such goodness to your servant as a sign of the abundance of your mercies.

What else might I say to you? I can only humble myself in your sight, recalling my weakness and sinfulness. Among all the wonders of Heaven and earth, none is comparable to you. Your works are good, your judgments are fair, and it is by your providence that the universe is governed. To you, O Wisdom of the Father, be praise and glory given. Let my soul, my tongue, and all creatures join in praising and blessing you!

xxii. *Keep in remembrance God's many gifts to you.*
THE DISCIPLE:

O Lord, open my heart to know your laws; teach me to walk within the bounds of your commandments. Give me the gift to understand your will for me, and to recall with good reverence and thankfulness your benefits toward me. For I desire, henceforth, to give you worthy thanks for them, be they general or special. Yet I know that, even for the least of your blessings to me, I am unable to give you sufficent thanks for your favors. The very least of your favors toward me is more than I deserve; and when I consider your perfection and its greatness, my spirit is overwhelmed.

Whatever any of us possesses in body or soul, outwardly or inwardly, naturally or supernaturally, is possessed as a gift from you; all blessings are given by you, proclaiming your bounty, mercy, and goodness—you, from whom we receive everything that is good. Even though some receive more and others less, all gifts nevertheless belong to you; and apart from you, there are no blessings to be obtained.

One who has been spectacularly blessed by you cannot claim to have deserved the glory, nor think himself superior to others, nor lord it over them. It is the person who presumes nothing for himself but most humbly and devoutly offers you his thanks who is the greater and better. So too, the one who reckons himself the least of men and considers himself most unworthy of your favor is most suited to receive your finest gifts.

Yet one who has received fewer of your blessings ought not to lose heart or fall into grief, nor look enviously upon those who have been more enriched by them. Instead, let him turn his mind to you and praise your goodness for sharing your favors so generously, freely, and willingly, without regard to a person's worldly estate.

All things were created by you, Lord, and therefore in all things you are to be praised. You best know what is good to give to each person, and why one should have less and another more. That is for you to judge, rather than for us; for you alone can know each person's true deserving.

For that reason, O Lord, I consider it a blessing that I do not have those blessings which are esteemed and praised by popular opinion. One who looks rightly at his own poverty and personal unworthiness will not see a reason for discouragement or sadness, but will be gladdened by this thought: that you, O Lord, have chosen the poor and the humble and the despised of this world to be your own close friends and servants. We see this most clearly in your own Apostles, whom you have appointed to be princes over all the earth.

Did they not live in this world simply and humbly, free of malice and deceit, happy to suffer rejection for your name's sake? What the worldly rejected, they embraced with deep affection.

So it is that when a person loves you and acknowledges you as the giver of all blessings, nothing is more appealing than to accept whatever your will may be and whatever you may please to decree for the sake of eternity. Such a person would take so much contentment and comfort from that thought, that it would seem as desirable to be the least as another person might think it to be the greatest. He would be as content to be in last place as in first; to be a despised, rejected person, notable neither in name nor in character, as to be honored above others and considered greater than they.

For *your* will and *your* glory ought to be esteemed above all things, and are a source of more comfort and joy than all the benefits that any of us on earth has already received or may yet receive.

xxiii. *There are four ways to inner peace.*

THE VOICE OF CHRIST:

My child, I shall teach you now the path to peace and true liberty.

THE DISCIPLE:

Lord, I pray you, teach me the way, for I would be delighted to have your counsel.

THE VOICE OF CHRIST:

Make it your first desire, my child, to prefer to do what another wills rather than what you desire.

Second, make it your goal always to have less rather than more.

Third, seek for yourself the lowest place, where you will be inferior to all others.

Fourth, make it your wish and constant prayer that the will of God may find its fulfillment through you.

You will find that one who lives in that manner, lives within the borders of peace and rest.

THE DISCIPLE:

Lord, this brief counsel includes much that leads to perfection. Few in words, but full of significance and fruitfulness. If I could keep faithful to these precepts, I would have little reason to become upset. Whenever I find myself to be despondent or frustrated, I find also that I had drawn apart from your counsel. May you, who can do all things and who long to see the good of my soul, increase your grace to me so that I may accept your tutelage and work out my own salvation.

—A Prayer against Evil Thoughts

O Lord my God, do not hold yourself far from me. Look for ways to assist me, Lord. Many temptations and fears have risen up against me, tormenting my soul. How shall I pass through them unscathed? Or how to cause them to collapse?

You said: "I shall go before you, and shall humble the great ones of the earth; I shall open the doors of the prison and reveal unto you my secrets" (Isaiah 45.2-3). O Lord, do as you have said; let all my evil thoughts flee at the sight of your face approaching.

My single hope or consolation is to flee to you whenever I am troubled; to place my trust in you; to call upon you from the center of my heart; and to wait patiently for your consoling touch.

—A Prayer for Illumination of Mind

O merciful Jesus, enlighten me with your clear, shining, inner light; chase away every trace of darkness residing in my heart. Subdue my wandering thoughts, and crush into pieces the temptations that most fiercely attack me. Fight vigorously for my sake, and conquer my "evil beasts"—I mean, the alluring desires of my flesh. I look for peace obtained through your power, and I long to hear your praise abundantly resounding in a holy court (that is, in my purified conscience). Command once more the wind and the storm. Say unto the sea, "Be still!" Say to the north wind: "Do not blow!" And then there will be a great calm within me.

Send out your light and your truth, that they may illuminate the earth. Unless you enlighten me, I am like an earth empty and formless. Pour down your grace from above; let heavenly dew penetrate my heart. Supply me with fresh streams of devotion, watering the face of this earth so that it may bring forth good and tasty fruits.

Lift up my mind; it is pressed down by the weight of my sins. Draw all my desires Heavenward, so that, once I have tasted the sweetness of everlasting happiness, I may find it distasteful to concern myself with earthly things.

Pluck me away and deliver me from the passing consolations that others may provide me. No created thing

*can fully comfort me or satisfy my longings. Bind yourself
to me with an unbreakable cord of love; you alone can
satisfy the one who loves you. Such a one must think all
else empty and frivolous.*

xxiv. *Do not be inquisitive about others' private lives.*

THE VOICE OF CHRIST:

My child, do not spend time in idle curiosity or as-
sociated anxieties. What can the this-and-that of such
things mean to you? Instead, follow me.

What concern is it of yours that so-and-so has done
or said such-and-such? You will not be asked to answer
for others' behavior, but only for your own! So why
should you involve yourself in others' affairs?

Is it not obvious that I know each person truly and
see all things done under the sun? Do I not also know
the circumstances of each person's life, how each
thinks, what each desires, and with what intentions
each one lives? Refer all things to me, therefore, and
keep yourself gently at peace. Let those whose lives are
without peace be as unpeaceful as they choose to make
themselves. Whatever they might do or say is a weight
that they fashion for themselves. They cannot deceive
me.

Do not long to live under the shadow of fame, or desire to be recognized by many, or even to have the close
friendship of many. Such desires keep the heart from
seeking its proper goal, and darken it. If you would but
look for my approach and open to me the doors of your
heart, I would willingly share my counsel with you and

reveal my secrets to you. Be prudent, watchful in prayer, and humble in all your activities.

xxv. *Peace of heart and spiritual progress are found in doing the will of God.*

THE VOICE OF CHRIST:

My child, this I have said: "Peace I leave with you. My peace I give to you. Not as the world gives, do I give unto you" (John 14.27). Peace is what each person desires; but not everyone cares for the ways by which true peace is found. My peace is known to those who are humble and gentle of heart. Your own peace can be found only with much patience. If you heed my words and follow my counsel, you will enjoy a full peace.

THE DISCIPLE:

Lord, what should I do, then?

THE VOICE OF CHRIST:

In everything, keep watch over what you say and what you do; and train yourself to choose whatever behavior will be pleasing to me. Do not desire or seek anything besides me. But as for the words and actions of others, do not judge rashly or involve yourself in matters that do not concern you. In that way you will keep yourself from almost all inner turmoil.

Understand, however, that it is not granted you in this life to be entirely free of discomfort or emotional and physical strain. Such freedom belongs to the state of Eternal Rest.

If you should feel no heaviness of heart, do not suppose that you have found true peace. If you are unaware of any attack on yourself by any foe, do not assume that all is well. For "to be perfect" does not mean "to have everything as one would wish it."

So too, if you find yourself caught up in a state of strong devotion and sweet feelings, do not congratulate yourself on your superiority. One who truly loves virtue is not to be identified on that basis; nor do the spiritual progress and perfection of a person consist in such things.

THE DISCIPLE:

In what do they consist, Lord?

THE VOICE OF CHRIST:

They consist in making a complete offering of yourself, with your whole heart, to the will of God. They do *not* involve your seeking to have what you think is yours, whether it be something small or large, something temporal or eternal. Only in that way can you preserve your peace of soul, or be thankful in times of adversity as well as in times of good fortune, and recognize all things in a clear light.

If you can steel your hopefulness to bravery and perseverance, so that your heart is prepared to suffer even more when all spiritual consolations are withdrawn from it, and if you do not complain that you do not deserve to suffer so much, but instead continue to acknowledge the justice of my providence and to praise my holy name—then will you be walking along the right path, the path of peace. Then too will your hope of seeing me face to face, in joy, be assured. If you can bring yourself to hold your self-interest in contempt, you will experience an overflowing peace, as much as you can experience during your earthly life.

xxvi. *You will sooner free your mind from worldly cares by humble prayer than by any mental effort.*

THE DISCIPLE:

O Lord, it is characteristic of one who is perfect to keep constantly in mind the things of Heaven, and thus be able to pass carelessly, so to speak, though the cares of this world. Not that such a one would lack all feeling, but that, having kept free from excessive attachment to any material thing, his mind would enjoy a special freedom.

My most merciful God, I ask you to keep me free from the cares of this life, so that they do not entangle me; from the needs and desires of my body, so that its pleasure does not become a trap for me; and from all enemies of my soul, so that troubles do not weaken and overthrow me. I do not ask for freedom from those things which vain and worldly people seek to avoid, but from those punishing miseries common to all humanity; for they distract the soul of your servant and burden it, often preventing it from enjoying the liberty it constantly desires.

O my God, whose sweetness is beyond my words to describe, grant that all bodily pleasures may seem to me sour; for they draw me away from desiring things eternal and, by a kind of deceit, draw me toward some nearer, present good. Keep me, dear Lord, from being overcome by flesh and blood; let not the world and its passing glory distract me; nor let the devil, subtle deceiver, undo me.

Grant me three wishes: the strength to resist; the patience to endure; and the constancy to persevere.

Rather than any worldly comfort, soothe me with the ointment of your Spirit; empty me of bodily passion, and fill me instead with love for your name.

Food and drink, clothing and other needs of the body—these are nothing but distractions for the devout soul. I pray that I make but limited use of what refreshes the body, for otherwise I may fall into the habit of pampering myself. It is not lawful to neglect entirely the needs of the body, for one must sustain one's natural life; but the same law forbids self-indulgence and pleasure-for-pleasure's sake, for that is to make the flesh rebel against the spirit. So I ask that your hand guide me in such matters, keeping me from wandering in either direction toward excess.

xxvii. *Selfish love does most to keep us from the Highest Good.*

THE VOICE OF CHRIST:

My child, you do well to give your whole self to the Source of all, and reserve nothing of yourself to yourself.

For you must know this: what does you most harm in this world is your love for yourself.

The love and affection you have for anything more or less cause it to become part of you. If your love is pure, honest, and reasonable, you will be able to keep yourself from becoming a slave to material things. Do not long to have what is unlawful for you to have; nor to possess anything that may compromise your conscience or destroy your inner liberty.

Is it not strange that you have not committed yourself wholly to me, from the bottom of your heart, along with all your desires and possessions? Why do you complain, so vainly, about your lot? Why do your insignificant concerns bring you so much weariness? If you would put your trust in my good will, you would have no sense of loss at all. But if you think you must have this or that, or be in this place or that, in order to feel successful and happy, you will never know any rest or peace of mind. In every worldly good, you will find something lacking; in every place, there will be someone to cross you.

Human happiness does not lie in obtaining material things and increasing their number, but in despising them and rooting out from the heart all desire for them. And this is true not only of money and wealth, but of honor and of desire for worldly fame—all of which pass away in this world. Without spiritual fervor, your being in one place rather than in another will bring you small comfort; and the peace you seek from external things will quickly fade. Unless you base your life steadfastly on me, your heart will have no firm foundation; and then you may change, indeed, but will never be the better for it! For in seeking to take advantage of every worldly opportunity, you will only find yourself in the sort of situation you would ordinarily flee from, or worse.

—A Prayer for a Clean Heart and Holy Wisdom

Strengthen me, O God, by the grace of the Holy Spirit. May I be strengthened with might inwardly, and my heart be emptied of vain cares and sorrow; may I refrain from being caught up in multiple longings, whether they be for frivolous or precious things, and instead look upon all things as passing away, and on myself also as among those things which will soon pass away. For nothing is permanent under the sun; here, all things are but vanities and vexation of soul. Wise is the one who sees them so! Lord, grant me also holy wisdom, so that I may learn to seek and find you above all, to desire and love you above all, and to see all else as being, as it is, at your wise disposal. Grant me prudence, to avoid any who flatter me and endure patiently any who contradict me. For it is a large part of wisdom to remain unmoved by the wind of words, and to give no ear to the evil, flattering siren: and thus we shall continue faithful to the way we have begun.

xxviii. *Be not troubled if others speak ill of you.*

THE VOICE OF CHRIST:

My child, do not be grieved if others have a low opinion of you or speak slightingly about you. You ought to be the most severe critic of yourself, and think of yourself as weaker than any other person.

If you care for the inner man, you will attach little importance to the quick-fading words of others. It is a great prudence to keep silence in an evil moment, and to turn yourself inwardly toward me; in that way you will not be troubled by how others judge you.

Do not look for your peace in what comes from the tongues of others; whether their judgment of you is faulty or sound, you are not thereby changed into a different person. Where are true peace and glory to be found, if not in me? The person who neither lives to please human opinion, nor lives in fear of displeasing others, is the person who will know much peace.

From such misplaced love and vain fear, all emotional upset and mental confusion come.

xxix. *In a time of trouble, call upon the Lord and bless his name.*

THE DISCIPLE:

May your name, O Lord, be forever blessed; for it is by your will that this present trial and tribulation has come upon me. Unable to escape it, I flee to you for help and ask you to turn it to my benefit.

Lord, in my affliction, my heart is upset and troubled by this suffering. And yet, beloved Father, what shall I pray for? I am caught up in distress; save me from this hour.

Yet why have I come into this hour, except that you may be glorified when I shall have become much humbled and then be delivered by you? May it please you, Lord, to deliver me. Poor wretch that I am, what can

I do, or where can I go, without your assistance?

Teach me patience, O Lord, even now in this time of desperation. If you help me, my God, I shall not fear—no matter how terribly I may be afflicted.

So what shall I, in the midst of trouble, say but: *Lord, your will be done.* For I have deserved to be afflicted and burdened, and therefore ought to bear it, yes even with patience, until the storm passes and all is well again—or even better!

The might of your hand can remove this temptation from me or lessen its force, so that I do not sink and drown. In times past, you have often come to my assistance, O my God, my Mercy. The more danger I am in, the more easily can your right hand, O Most High, deliver me.

xxx. *Call on the Lord when you are tempted; trust in his mercy.*

THE VOICE OF CHRIST:

My child, I am the Lord, who gives strength in the day of trial. Whenever you feel overwhelmed, come unto me. It is your slowness in turning to me in prayer that most keeps you from heavenly comforting. You prefer to look first for comfort and consolation in external things, and only then do you come a beggar to me. Inevitably you find that those external comforts bring you little profit, and then you remember that it is I who rescue those who trust in me. Apart from me, you will find no lasting help, no useful counsel, no lasting medicine.

After you have recovered your breath with the passing of the storm, renew your strength in the rays of my mercy; for I stand ready to renew you, not only completely but abundantly and beyond your need.

Is there anything that is difficult for me to accomplish? Am I like one who promises but does not do what he promises? Where is your faith? Stand firm. Persevere. Take courage and be patient. In due time, my comfort will come to you.

Wait for me. Wait, I say, and I shall come and care for your needs. It is but a temptation that troubles you; it is a selfish fear that frightens you. What else can you expect from worrying about what the future might bring for you, except sorrow after sorrow? "Sufficient for the day is the evil thereof" (Matthew 6.34).

To be disturbed or pleased about what the future might bring you is both useless and vain. Your expectations may never come to pass. How typically human it is to be deceived about the imagined future! It is a sign that the mind is weak, easy prey to the suggestions of the Enemy. Satan's only desire is to deceive and delude you—whether by truth or falsity, he cares not, nor whether by affections for present things or by fear of the future.

So do not let your heart be troubled or fearful. Trust in me; be confident of my mercy. Sometimes, when you think you are farthest from me, I am actually closest to you. Just when you think you have lost nearly everything, you are closest to gaining a great reward.

Do not think "all is lost" when your hopes are dashed. Do not let your present feelings be the measure of your present state. And no matter how grief enters your life, do not abandon yourself to it, as if you had lost all hope of escaping it.

It may happen that, for a time, I shall send you a trial or even withhold from you the comforting you seek. Do not think yourself completely abandoned, but consider instead that that is the way to the kingdom of Heaven. It certainly is better that you and my other servants endure frustration and trials than that you have your every desire fulfilled.

I know the secret longings of your heart. But I also know that your welfare is better assured if you are sometimes left in desert dryness, without the refreshment of spiritual sweetness. Otherwise you are likely to puff yourself up with prosperity and form an exaggerated opinion of yourself.

What I have given, I can take away; and what I take away, I can restore again, as I please. What I give is still mine; what I take away is nothing of your own. Every good gift, every perfect gift, is from me. If I send you some affliction—any sort of cross—do not fall into self-pity or let your heart despair. Quickly can I assist you and convert your sorrow to joy. In all things, I deal righteously with you and deserve to be praised by you.

If you are wise and give careful thought to what is true, you will never lapse into melancholy whenever an unhappiness befalls you. Instead, rejoice and give thanks. Indeed, you will do well to think this present time, when I afflict you with sorrows and do not spare you, a time of special joy. To my beloved disciples, I said: "As the Father has loved me, I also love you" (John 15.9). Clearly, I sent them out, not to earthly joy, but to severe persecution; not to honors, but to hatred; not to leisure, but to labor; not to rest, but to bring forth much fruit with patience. My child, keep these words in memory.

xxxi. *To draw close to your Creator, draw yourself away from attachment to creatures.*

THE DISCIPLE:

O Lord, I am much in need of an increase of grace if I am to reach that stage where no person, no creature, will hold me back from you. As long as any person or thing does so, I am not free to fly unto you. It was with such longing that the Psalmist said, "O that I had the wings of a dove, that I might fly away and be at rest!" (Psalm 55.6) Who could be more "at rest" than one who has but one goal in view? And who could be more "free" than one who desires nothing on the earth?

A person ought to pass above all earthly creatures and even go "out of himself" and stand, in a sort of ecstasy of mind, so as to see that you, the Creator of all, have no equal among your creatures.

Truly, too, unless a person be free from all creatures, he will be unable to devote his mind fully to divine things. For that reason, one finds few contemplatives in this world. There are few whose wisdom enables them to detach themselves fully from perishable creatures.

Much grace is required to reach that contemplative plane; it is grace that elevates the soul, and carries it, so to speak, above itself.

Unless a person is elevated in soul and freed from creaturely attachments, and thus wholly united with God, his knowledge and his attainments have no great value. On the contrary, he who sees greatness in anything besides the one and only infinite and eternal Good will long lie small and groveling here below.

Whatever is not God, is nothing, and ought to be thought of as nothing. The wisdom of an enlightened and devout person is much greater than that of a learned and diligent scholar. Learning that flows downward from God's influence is far nobler than anything the mere wit of man can painstakingly discover.

Many persons desire to be contemplatives, but they will not undergo the training that contemplation requires. Another obstacle for many is that they put too much emphasis on external appearances, and too little on perfectly mortifying their willfulness. I do not know why it is, or what spirit it is that leads us, or what pretence takes hold of us, but we who like to think of ourselves as "spiritual" persons are constantly busy and anxious about petty and passing concerns; and at the same time, we scarcely, if at all, give full thought to our spiritual concerns. If, briefly, we achieve a moment of interior reflection, we soon fall back into our usual state and fail to give our behavior close scrutiny. We do not examine where our affections truly lie, nor do we chide ourselves for the evil in our actions. The Great Deluge took place because "all mankind was corrupted" (Genesis 6.12). If our inner inclinations are much corrupted, it follows that our actions must also be corrupted; and the latter give evidence of the weakness within us. It is from a pure heart that one obtains the fruit of a good life.

We ask: How much has so-and-so done? But we are less concerned whether someone has acted from virtuous principle. We ask: Is he brave, rich, handsome, skillful? Is she a good writer, a good singer, a good employee? Seldom do we ask whether a person is poor in spirit, or patient and meek, or devout and spiritual.

The outward gifts of a person are the work of Nature; the inner, the work of Grace. The outer, natural man is often disappointed; the inner, spiritual man has his trust in God and therefore is never disappointed.

xxxii. *Put aside all your selfishness and self-love.*

THE VOICE OF CHRIST:

My child, you will not have perfect liberty until you renounce yourself completely. Those who only love themselves and seek whatever serves their self-interests are actually living in chains. They are grasping, inquisitive, gossipy persons; they seek after whatever is soft and comfortable, not the things of Jesus Christ; and they devote themselves to schemes and plans that are doomed to come to an end. For whatever is not of God will perish.

Keep this short but true saying in mind: "Give up all to obtain all." Cease to cater to your bodily appetites and you will find rest. Consider this counsel carefully; and when you have put it into practice, you will understand the truth of all things.

THE DISCIPLE:

O Lord, what you ask is not the work of a day, nor child's play; yet in this saying is included the formula for perfection for those who seek to live a religious life.

THE VOICE OF CHRIST:

My child, do not be soon dismayed or turn aside when you hear the way to spiritual perfection. Rather, stir yourself to better things, and at least resolve to make them your goal. This is what I wish for you: that you had already arrived at the point where you no longer were a lover of yourself but stood ever-ready to serve my will—and the will of those whom I have placed in position of religious authority over you. Then would you be greatly pleasing to me, and all your life would pass in joy and peace.

As it is, you still have many attachments to part with; and unless you entirely place yourself at my service, you will never attain the goal you most desire. "I counsel you to buy of me gold tried by fire, in order that you may become rich" (Revelation 3.18). In other words, be rich in heavenly wisdom, which spurns underfoot whatever is mean and low. Put little faith in worldly wisdom; and be not over-anxious to please others or yourself.

I have said: trade those things which are commonly thought of as valuable and precious for something commonly thought of as of little value. Truly, heavenly wisdom does seem to be of little value, of small account, and nearly forgotten among humankind. Such wisdom has no high opinion of itself and seeks no earthly recognition or fame. Many, of course, do praise it loudly, but keep themselves far from it in their lives. Yet it is the "pearl of great price" (Matthew 13.46), hidden from many.

xxxiii. *Keep the true end of your life—God—constantly in sight, despite distractions that might draw you away from him.*

THE VOICE OF CHRIST:

My child, place no trust in your feelings; one emotion tells you one thing now, but another is soon telling you something else. Throughout your life, you will find yourself changing, despite your wishes. One moment you will feel merry, and in a little while, sad; one time at peace, another time, troubled; now devout, later spiritually bored; one minute enthusiastic, the next fatigued; today serious, tomorrow frivolous.

The person who is wise and well instructed in spiritual things stands fast against the wavering of the emotions. He pays no more heed to his passing feelings than to the direction a fickle wind is blowing. His mind is focused on the right, and best, end. In that manner he succeeds in remaining steadfast and unshaken. As he passes through many contrary forces, he keeps his eyes fixed firmly on me.

The more pure he keeps the "eye of his intention," the greater his constancy in passing through the several kinds of storms that assault him. In many, however, the intention that governs the eye weakens and grows dim, being drawn aside to some passing object that meets them with a promise of pleasure.

It is truly rare to find a person wholly free of any blemish caused by self-seeking. Many Jews went to the home of Martha and Mary not only because Jesus was there, but to see Lazarus also.

The eye of our intention is therefore to be purified, so that it is unbending and rightly directed. Beyond all the objects that might come within view, it is to be directed toward me.

xxxiv. *Those who love God above all things can love all things for his sake.*

THE DISCIPLE:

"Behold my God and my All!" What more could I wish for? What greater happiness could I desire? O sweet and delicious name—for so it seems to one who loves the Word rather than the world and the things in the world. *My God and my All*—to one who understands, this is enough to say. One who loves God takes delight in repeating the words often.

When you are present, Lord, all things bring us delight; but when you are absent, they irritate us. Quietness of heart, abiding peace, and festive joy are your gifts. It is you who help us see good in our circumstances of life, and to praise you for them. Not for long can anything please us apart from you. Before anything can seem pleasant and tasteful to us, your grace and the seasoning of your wisdom must be with us.

What thing is there that could displease one whose

pleasure is in you? Or how could anything be pleasing to one who has no taste for you?

Worldly people who are considered "wise" and those who pamper the flesh utterly lack your wisdom; the former are full of vanity, the latter, full of death. But those who follow you, through contempt for worldly things, through mortification of the flesh, are truly wise. They have been brought over from vanity to truth, from flesh to spirit. They have a well-developed taste for God; and any good they find in creatures they see as an occasion for praising their Creator.

Yet how vast a difference there is between their delight in the Creator and in the creature; between their delight in what is Eternal and what is temporal; between Light uncreated and light reflected.

O Everlasting Light, more brilliant than any created source of light, shine forth your bright rays from above and let them penetrate to the center of my heart. Purify, cheer, enlighten, and enliven my soul and all its powers, so that I may cling to you with surpassing joy and jubilation.

Oh, when will come that blessed and longed-for hour when you will fully satisfy me by your presence and be all-in-all to me? Until this gift is granted me, I shall lack fullness of joy. But alas, the "old man" still lives on in me, not yet wholly crucified, not yet wholly dead. He still battles strongly against the soul, stirring up inner conflict, preventing the kingdom of the soul from being at peace.

But you who rule the might of the sea and calm the

motions of the waves, rise up and come to my aid. Scatter the forces that wage war against me; crush them with your might. Make known your marvelous works, I pray, and let your right hand be honored. For I have no other hope or refuge than in you, O Lord my God.

xxxv. *There is no refuge from temptation in this life.*

THE VOICE OF CHRIST:

My child, in this life, you will never be entirely secure; as long as you live, you will need spiritual armor. You live among enemies; you are attacked both right and left. If you do not raise the shield of patience to defend yourself, you will not long go unwounded. And if your heart is not fixed firmly on me, and if you have not desired to endure your sufferings for my sake, you will find the heat of battle unbearable; and you will not win the palm of the blessed.

Move bravely through whatever opposes you. Take a strong hand against anything that challenges you. For to the one who overcomes temptation, manna is given; while to the weak-hearted, the "reward" is much misery.

If you work to be at rest in this life, how will you ever obtain the everlasting rest you desire? Instead of looking for ways to find rest for yourself, learn well the art of patience. The peace you seek—true peace—is to be sought in Heaven; not on earth or in your fellow man or any other creature, but in God only.

Your love for God should be your motive for undergoing all things cheerfully: all labor, all pain, all temptation, all frustration, all anxiety, every necessity and infirmity, injury and scorn, disgrace and humiliation, confusion and correction. Such things are a source of virtue. They are the trials of a follower of Christ; and they shape a heavenly crown for you. For your short time of trial, I grant an eternal reward. The mortal life of confusion you now experience I shall crown with everlasting glory.

Do you suppose that you will have my spiritual consolations whenever you desire them? My saints had no such privilege, though they endured many temptations, trials, and periods of feeling entirely abandoned. Yet they bore up patiently, trusting in God rather than in themselves. They knew that the sufferings of this life could not be compared to the glory that awaited them in the next. So why should you expect to receive instantly what many others, despite their sorrows and hard labors, have hardly obtained?

Wait, then, for the Lord. Persevere. Be of good courage. Do not lose your trust in God. Do not retreat, but dedicate yourself, body and soul, to his glory. The reward I give is most generous. And I shall be at your side through every trial.

xxxvi. *Do not judge yourself according to the standards of worldly opinion.*

THE VOICE OF CHRIST:

My child, fix your heart firmly on the Lord. If your conscience finds you dutiful and innocent, pay no attention to how others may judge you. If you suffer from others' ill opinion of you, count it a good and happy sign. What others think will not sadden a humble heart, one that trusts in God rather than in itself.

Most people tend to talk too much; hence it is unwise to place much confidence in them. Besides, you will find it impossible to please everybody! Saint Paul tried to please all "in the Lord," and to become "all things to all men," yet he never thought the opinion that others had of him was of much importance. He did as much as he could do for the enlightenment and salvation of others; and there was no way for him to keep others from judging, and even despising, him. He therefore committed his labors to the judgment of God, who knew all. When others spoke unjustly or foolishly or deceitfully about him or laid accusations against him, he allowed his patience and humility to be his defence. The only times he did confront and answer his critics were when his silence might have scandalized the weak.

Who are you, then, that you should fear the judgment of mortals, who are here today and gone tomorrow? If you feared God as you should, you would not cower from the threats of human tongues. How can the words and threats of another person do you harm? The person he hurts is himself; and whoever he be, he will not escape the judgment of God.

For your part, keep God within sight and do not do battle against peevish talk. Even if it seems that your reputation now suffers, and undeserved shame is cast upon you, do not be a grumbler or tarnish your crown by any impatience. Instead, lift up your eyes to me, in Heaven, for I can deliver you from every shame and abuse, and render to each person according to his works.

xxxvii. *By dying to selfishness, we live eternally with Christ.*

THE VOICE OF CHRIST:

My child, abandon yourself and you will find me. Set aside your willfulness and seek no personal aggrandizement; you will then be the gainer. For the moment you surrender all concern for self, abundant grace will be yours so long as you do not fall back into selfish ways.

THE DISCIPLE:

Lord, how often shall I surrender, and what does "abandoning" myself entail?

THE VOICE OF CHRIST:

Your self-surrender must be constant—yes, hour by hour; and you must abandon both small and large self-indulgence, with no exception. It is my desire that you be stripped of your whole natural self. Unless you discard from you every trace of self-will, inwardly as well as outwardly, you cannot be entirely mine, nor I yours. The sooner you do so, the better it will be for you; and the more successfully and sincerely you do so, the more pleasing I shall find you, and the greater will be your gain.

There are those who mortify themselves, but who leave themselves with a few exceptions; not putting all their trust in God, they continue to be concerned about providing for their "needs." And there are also those who do offer themselves entirely to me, but who afterward, when difficulties come, fall back into their former ways. Consequently they make no progress along the path of virtue.

Those who fall into either of those two groups never reach the liberty of a pure heart. They never enjoy the favor of my sweetest friendship—unless, of course, they surrender themselves entirely and offer themselves daily as a sacrifice to me. Until they do that, there can be no lasting or fruitful union between us.

You have heard me say often, and again I say to you: "Deny yourself" (Matthew 26.24). Surrender your very self, and you will enjoy a deep inner peace.

Give up "all for all." Ask for nothing; require nothing in return. Live entirely and unhesitatingly in me, and you will possess me. You will then be free of heart, and no darkness will trample you down.

Let it be your whole objective, prayer, and desire, that you may be stripped of every trace of selfishness and may follow Jesus in complete simplicity of life; and that you may in that way die to yourself and live eternally in me.

Only thus can you rid yourself of all foolish desires, all petty upsets, and all needless worries. Then will your silly apprehensions leave you; then your excessive self-love will die.

xxxviii. *Accept full responsibility for your own affairs, turning to God in time of danger.*

THE VOICE OF CHRIST:

My child, wherever you are and whatever your labor

or occupation, keep yourself inwardly free and take charge of your behavior. Keep your daily affairs under your rule, rather than letting them govern your life. You must be lord and master of your own actions, not a slave to your work. Live like a free-born person, a faithful Hebrew, passing over to claim the condition and freedom of the sons of God. For they, though they stand on things present, contemplate things eternal. With the left eye they take note of the passing affairs of the world; with their right, the things of Heaven.

They do not succumb and allow temporal affairs to consume their lives; instead, they govern their daily affairs in accord with what is ordained and appointed by God, the great Workmaster. He has left nothing unordered in his creation.

If you likewise, in all the circumstances of your life, remain steadfast, and if you do not judge what you see and hear by outward appearances or appeal, but constantly, like Moses, enter the Tabernacle to ask the Lord's counsel: then it will happen, from time to time, that the Divine Oracle will speak to you and instruct you concerning many things, present and future.

Moses always presented himself in the Tabernacle for help in resolving doubts and questions. When assaulted by dangers or threatened by human wickedness, he fled to prayer for help. So ought you to do, taking refuge in the private chamber of your heart, earnestly calling on God's favor.

We read that Joshua and the children of Israel did not ask the Lord's counsel beforehand but, trusting too much in fair words, deluded themselves with their own false piety and were deceived by the Gibeonites (Joshua 9.14).

xxxix. *Do not overly concern yourself with practical affairs.*

THE VOICE OF CHRIST:

My child, place all your desires before me, and in good time I shall deal with them. Wait patiently for my decision, and you will find that it serves your best interest.

THE DISCIPLE:

Lord, gladly do I commit all my cares to you; for my own abilities cannot encompass them.

I wish that I did not concern myself so much about what the future might bring me, but instead could resign myself to accepting your good pleasure.

THE VOICE OF CHRIST:

My child, it often happens that someone will struggle long and hard for what he desires; and then, once he has achieved it, his interest passes on to something else. Human interests seldom remain long fixed on one thing; instead, they move today toward one goal, tomorrow toward another. Hence it is a great advantage for a person to surrender his self-will even in little things.

It is precisely by such self-denial that a person brings himself most benefit; for he who has denied himself lives in both freedom and security. Nevertheless, the Ancient Enemy sets himself most vigorously against those who are virtuous. He does not cease to tempt them; day and night he lies in wait to trap the unwary, and catch them, if he can, in his net of deceit.

"Watch and pray," as the Lord says, "so that you do not succumb to temptation" (Matthew 26.41).

xl. *Apart from God, there is nothing good in you, nothing from which you can take glory.*

THE DISCIPLE:

"Lord, what is man, that you are mindful of him, or the son of man, that you visit him?" (Psalm 8.5). How has man deserved that you should grant him your favor?

On what grounds could I complain, O Lord, if you were to forsake me? Or if you do not grant my petitions, how could I in justice claim to be wronged?

This, rather, may I think and say: Lord, I am as nothing. I can do nothing. Of myself, I have nothing that is good. In all aspects, I am a decaying thing, ever tending toward nothingness. Unless you be my help and inwardly refashion me, I grow increasingly lukewarm and fragmented.

But you, O Lord, remain always the same, and live forever—always good, always just, always holy. You do all things well, justly, and holily; and you order all things in wisdom.

I, on the other hand, am more likely to go backward than forward, and never remain in an unchanging condition, for I change with the seasons. Yet when it pleases you to stretch forth your hand in help, my condition quickly improves. Without any human assistance, you can help and strengthen me, so that my countenance ceases to change and my heart is turned toward you alone and is at rest.

If only I could once completely cast aside my desire for human comforts— either so that I could give my full effort to devotion, or because my needs impel me to search for you (for no mortal being can truly comfort me). Then I might well hope for your grace and rejoice in each gift of new consolation.

I give you my thanks—you, from whom all things come—whenever all goes well in my life. But in your eyes I must be all but nothing, a vain, wavering, and weak person. Of what then can I boast? On what basis can I ask to be respected? Is it that I am nothing? This thought too is completely foolish. Empty self-glory is truly an evil plague, the vainest of vanities, drawing a person away from real glory and robbing him of divine grace. For inasmuch as a person pleases himself, he is displeasing to you. Lusting after the adulation of others, he deprives himself of the true virtues.

Real glory and holy rejoicing belong to the person who glories in you rather than in himself; who rejoices in your name rather than in his own virtue; and who takes no delight in any creature.

Praised be your name, O Lord, not mine. May your works be proclaimed, not mine—unless it be for your sake. Let your holy name be blessed, but let no portion of human praise be given to me. My glory is in you, who are the joy of my heart. In you shall I glory and rejoice all the day; as for myself, I shall glory only in my infirmities. Let the Jewish leaders who sought Jesus' death "honor one another" (John 5.44). I shall look for that honor which comes from God alone.

In truth, all human glory and worldly honor and rank—compared to your eternal glory—are worthless and foolish.

To you alone, my God, my Truth and my Mercy, O Blessed Trinity, be praise, honor, power, and glory forever and ever.

xli. *Seek a lasting honor in Heaven rather than a temporary one on earth.*

THE VOICE OF CHRIST:

My child, if you see others honored and promoted while you are scorned and kept down, pay no attention. Lift up your heart to Heaven—to me—and the low opinion others may have of you will not cause you grief.

THE DISCIPLE:

Lord, we live in blindness and are easily misled by our own vanity. If I see myself as I truly am, I cannot say that anyone has ever *under*estimated me; so I can hardly complain when I stand before you. Because I have often sinned seriously against you, it is only just that all other creatures should be hostile toward me. Shame and contempt are my just deserts; but yours are praise, honor, and glory. So unless I resign myself, with a cheerful willingness, to be despised and neglected by all others, and to be reckoned as in no way notable, I shall enjoy neither inner peace nor stability, neither spiritual enlightenment nor perfect union with you.

xlii. *Do not expect your fellow creatures to help you know peace of heart.*

THE VOICE OF CHRIST:

My child, if you depend on one other person for your happiness, because you have come to esteem that person and have become dependent on his or her company each day, you will find yourself entrapped and easily hurt. But if instead your happiness lies in seeking the everliving and eternal Truth, the desertion or death of a close friend will not overly grieve you. Your esteem for a friend ought to be based on me; it is for my sake that you ought to love a friend, no matter who your friend may be, no matter how dear your friend may be to you. Apart from me, a friendship has no strength, no lasting-power; nor can any love be called pure or true if it is not knit together by me.

You should therefore let your merely "natural" affections for your close friends die, and live as if, so far as you are concerned, you would rather be without human comforting. A person approaches the nearer to God, the farther he or she withdraws from earthly comforts. In the same way, the more humble a person is, and the less worthy he is in his own eyes, the higher he ascends toward God. But the person who prides himself about any talent or accomplishment sets up a barrier so that God's grace cannot come to him; for the grace of the Holy Spirit looks only for the humble-hearted.

If you could entirely destroy your self-will, and detach yourself from all worldly affection, I might consider myself obliged to fill you to overflowing with my powerful grace. It is when you depend on creature comforts that the blessing of God is withdrawn from you.

In all things, then, learn how to overcome your willfulness, for the sake of your Creator. You will in that way obtain divine knowledge. If you love or esteem anything too much—no matter how insignificant it might seem—you corrupt the soul by holding her apart from the Creator.

xliii. *Worldly knowledge is of no value compared to heavenly wisdom.*

THE VOICE OF CHRIST:

My child, do not let common human opinion, no matter how cleverly or persuasively it is expressed, be your guide. "For the kingdom of God does not consist in talk but in virtue" (1 Corinthians 4.20). Attend to my words; they stir up the heart and enlighten the mind; they awaken repentance and are a source of abundant consolation.

Read the word of God, not in order to appear more learned or more wise than others, but so as to waken sorrow for your sins. Such sorrow will bring you more benefit than much knowledge on many difficult subjects.

No matter how much you have read and learned, you will always need to return to one Beginning and Principle of knowledge. It is I who teach a person true knowledge. For I give to small children a clearer understanding than they can be taught by human teachers. One to whom I speak will soon be wise and will enjoy much spiritual profit.

Let those beware who busy themselves about learning the affairs of others and give little thought to how they should serve me! The time will come when the Teacher of teachers, Christ the Lord of Angels, will appear and hear the lessons of all—that is, examine the consciences of all. Then will he search Jerusalem with candles, revealing the things hidden in darkness, stilling the debates of human tongues.

I am he who, in an instant, can raise a humble mind to understand more about eternal Truth than one could get from ten years of scholarly study. My teaching is accomplished without the din of words, without the clash of opinions, without the ambition of honor, and without the wrestling that argumentation entails. I am he who teaches the human mind to despise earthly things, to hold present things in contempt, to seek after eternal things and develop a taste for them, to flee honors, to endure offences, to place all hope in me, to have no desires apart from me, and especially to love me beyond all else.

There was once a person who, by loving me from the bottom of his heart, became instructed concerning divine truths and frequently spoke admirably about them. He made more intellectual progress by detaching himself from worldly things than he would have by studying insignificant questions. Yet to some persons I teach very common truths; to others, I give special insights. To some I reveal myself in signs and images; to others I appear as a bright light and reveal mysteries.

The "voice" of books is indeed a voice, but it does not teach every reader alike. It is I who, within each reader, am the teacher of truth, the understander of thoughts, the searcher of the heart, the prompter of action, granting to each person according to my judgment.

xliv. *Do not fill your life with things that do not concern your spiritual welfare.*

THE VOICE OF CHRIST:

My child, concerning many things, you have an obligation to be ignorant. You have an obligation also to look upon yourself as if you were "dead to the world," as if the whole world had been crucified so far as concerns you. So too, there are many things said to which you should turn a deaf ear; and in that way you will be able to be more mindful of those other things that contribute to your peace of mind.

You will be better off if you turn away your eyes from that which displeases you, if you leave others to their opinions rather than become a participant in quarrelsome arguments. If your relationship to God is as it should be and you keep his judgments in mind, you will find it quite easy to accept being "defeated."

THE DISCIPLE:

Lord, to what pass have we come? As you see, we human creatures complain about our every setback, and for a ridiculously small advantage we work and hustle. Meanwhile, we give no thought to the spiritual harm we do to ourselves, and we are scarcely able to turn our minds back to reconsider our spiritual condition. We give our attention to something that brings us little or no profit, while negligently ignoring what is truly necessary for our welfare. The whole person soon gets sidetracked into a preoccupation with external things; and unless he quickly recovers the way, he grows accustomed to abiding among externals, and willingly so.

xlv. *Be not quick to place your trust in others, for they are inclined to speak falsely.*

THE DISCIPLE:

Help me through my trials, Lord, for human assistance is unreliable. How often have I met with unfaithfulness in others, in whom I had placed a firm trust! Yet how often have I found it where I had least expected to find it! Foolish it is, therefore, to place one's hope in other human beings. In you, O God, do the righteous find salvation. Blessed be you, O Lord my God, in all the events of our lives! We are weak and shaky, quickly deceived and changeable.

Where is the person who is so careful and cautious that he never allows himself to be caught by any deceit or confusion? Only the one who trusts in you, O Lord, and seeks you with singleness of heart is least likely to fall into any tribulation. Yet if he should do so, no matter how much he may get caught up in it, he will soon be delivered by you or be comforted by you; for you will never abandon anyone who has a persevering hope in you.

Rare indeed is it that one has a faithful and loyal friend when one is in distress. Only you, O Lord, are completely faithful to your friends; and there is no one comparable to you.

How wise was that holy soul who said: "My mind is

firmly settled and grounded in Christ" (Saint Agatha). If only the same were true of me, I would not fear what others might do to harm me; and barbed words would not hurt me.

Where is the person who can foresee, and protect himself against, every future evil? Even when we do foresee events, they oftentimes bring us harm; so how can unforeseen evils not wound us terribly? But, wretch that I am, why have I not had better foresight concerning my own welfare? Why have I too readily put my faith in others?

But we are but human, and frail at that, even though many think and say we are "angels."

O Lord, whom then shall I trust? Whom, but you? You are the Truth who neither deceives nor can be deceived. On the other hand, "everyone in the world is a liar" (Romans 3.4), and weak, unreliable, and subject to fall—especially in speech. So one can hardly give instant assent even to statements that ring true.

How wise you were, Lord, to warn us to beware of placing our trust in others; to recall that a person's enemies may belong to his own household; and to withhold belief when we hear one say, "Lo, he is here," and another, "Lo, he is there."

My painful experience has been my teacher; would that it made me more cautious rather than more unwise! Someone says to me, "Be careful that you keep to yourself what I now tell you"—and then, while I keep to my promise and guard the secret, he himself cannot do what he asked me to promise to do, but soon betrays the confidence and goes on his way!

Protect me, Lord, from such troublemaking, irresponsible persons; let me not fall into their hands, and keep me from doing as they do. Grant that I may guard my words in truth and fidelity; and keep far from me deceitfulness of tongue. What I would not want done to myself I should make every effort to keep myself from doing.

How good it is, how favorable to peace, that I remain silent about others; that I be slow to believe what I am told about them, and that I be cautious in repeating what has been reported to me.

How good it is to reveal oneself to few, and instead seek after you, who see the heart.

How good it is not to let the words of others carry me away, but instead to desire that in body and soul I may act according to what pleases your will.

How much more safely one can keep heavenly grace by avoiding mere appearances or the seeking after whatever the worldly admire; and by working constantly to acquire godly zeal and the ability to amend one's life. Many persons have paid the price for seeking to publicize their virtue and win the praise of others. In this frail life—which, we are told, is all temptation and warfare—grace is truly profitable when we preserve it in silence.

xlvi. *Remember that you are truly judged only by God, not by human opinion.*

THE VOICE OF CHRIST:

My child, be firm and place your trust in me. For what are words but only words? They fly through the air, but they cannot hurt a stone. If your conscience calls you guilty, consider how you would gladly amend your life; if not, resolve to suffer willingly the lies of others, for God's sake. It is no brave thing to suffer sometimes from other's words, though you may not have the courage to endure hard lashing. Why is it that little annoyances pierce your heart, if not because you are still a servant to your body's desires and pay more attention to the opinion others have of you than you should. It is your fear of being scorned that makes you reluctant to be reprimanded for your faults and eager to protect yourself with excuses.

If you take a closer look at yourself, you will be forced to admit that the world still lives on in you, and that you have a foolish desire to please others. When you retreat from anything that might embarrass you or reveal your sins, you make it clear that you are neither humble nor truly dead to the world, and that the world has not been crucified in you. If you turn your ear to hear my word, you will not be troubled by even ten thousand words that others may speak against you. Even if every conceivable malicious accusation were leveled against you, how could it harm you if you let each pass you by, paying no more attention to any of it than you would to a speck of dust? Could any such accusation pluck a single hair from your head?

The person who doesn't tend his heart and keep God before his eyes is very vulnerable to a word of sharp criticism. But the person who trusts in me instead of relying on his own judgment will have no fear of human threats. For I am both the Judge and the Knower of all that is hidden. I know exactly how such-and-such a thing happened; I know from whom an injury comes, and who suffers it. It took place with my knowledge and my permission, so that "the thoughts of many hearts might be revealed" (Luke 2.35). I shall judge both the guilty and the innocent; but it is my wish to test them both beforehand in a hidden manner.

What people say is often deceiving. My judgment is ever true; it will stand and will never be reversed. It is usually hidden, and is shown to only a few, and then only by way of exception; but it never is in error, though the foolish-minded person may not think it "fair." Hence it is to me that you should turn before coming to judgment, rather than depending on your own opinions. No matter what God allows to befall a just person, he or she will not be disturbed. Even if falsely accused, a just person will not greatly care, nor parade boastfully if, thanks to the efforts of others, he or she is rightly vindicated. Such a one remembers that I search both hearts and motives, and that I do not judge mere appearances, the face that all can see. Indeed, it often happens that what human beings think praiseworthy is in my eyes condemnable.

THE DISCIPLE:

Lord God, strong, patient, and just judge, you well know the frailty and weakness of your human creatures: be my strength and my confidence, for my own conscience cannot fully sustain me. What I do not know about myself, you know. In complete humility

I should therefore submit to any blame laid on me. In your mercy, forgive me for ever having acted otherwise. And when my next trial comes, grant me the grace of complete perseverance. Your overflowing sympathy is better able to move me to seek pardon than any self-righteousness I might claim against the misgivings of my own conscience. And even if I knew of no accusation to bring against myself, I could not justly congratulate myself. In truth, except for your mercy, no human creature could ever, in your eyes, be justified.

xlvii. *Bear up under your present trials for the sake of eternal life.*

THE VOICE OF CHRIST:

My child, do not let the labors you have undertaken for my sake wear you down, and never become discouraged by your hardships. Let what I have promised you give you both strength and comfort in every circumstance of your life. I am well prepared to reward you, beyond what you hope for or deserve. Your present toils will not last long, and you will not always be burdened with your present griefs. Wait but a short while, and you will soon see your difficulties come to an end. The hour will come when all your labor and trouble will cease. Everything that passes away in time is of little value and shortlived.

Whatever you do, do conscientiously. Be a faithful worker in my vineyard, and I shall be your repayment. Write, read, chant, mourn, keep silence, pray, carry your crosses bravely: life everlasting in Heaven is worth these efforts, and greater efforts too.

In a day known only to the Lord, peace will come in to you, and it will be neither night nor day (as you now know them), but unceasing light, infinite brightness, lasting peace, and untroubled rest.

Then you will not have reason to say, "Who will rescue me from this mortal body?" (Romans 7.24). Nor will you cry out, "Alas, that my sojourn on earth is not at an end!" For then Death will be cast down headlong, and there will be unfailing salvation, freedom from anxiety, blessed joy, and a pleasing and noble society.

Would that you could see the everlasting crowns of the saints in Heaven, and also in what glory they now rejoice—they whom the world once thought ridiculous and intolerable—for then you would humble yourself indeed, even to the earth, and seek to be the least of all rather than have charge of a single other person!

Nor would you long to enjoy the world's comforts; rather, you would rejoice at the chance to endure your sufferings for God and think yourself best served if others rejected you completely.

If only you had cultivated a taste for such things and let it penetrate your heart, you could not dare to raise even a single complaint. Is it not true that present painful labors are to be endured for the sake of life eternal? It is no little thing, whether you gain or lose the Kingdom of God!

Lift your face to Heaven, therefore, and see me and all the saints with me, who in your world met with many conflicts; but now they are comforted and secure, and at rest, and will remain so with me forever in the Kingdom of my Father.

xlviii. *Use the difficulties of this present life as opportunities to store up treasure in Heaven.*

THE DISCIPLE:

O most blessed mansion of the City above! Most clear day of eternity, which darkness never shades, but Truth constantly illuminates! O day ever joyful, ever secure, and ever unchanging! Would that that day might appear to me, and that all things temporal were ended! To the saints, indeed, the eternal day shines with unwavering brightness. But to us who are still pilgrims on earth, it seems far off, as "through a glass darkly" (1 Corinthians 13.11).

The citizens of Heaven know how joyful their day is; but the banished children of Eve complain of the bitterness and tediousness of this earthly life. The days of this life are few and evil, full of sorrows and setbacks. Here, one is defiled by numerous sins, tangled by many passions, imprisoned by many fears, tormented with many cares, distracted by many curiosities, caught by many vanities, surrounded by many errors, worn down by many labors, weighed down by many temptations, weakened by pleasures, tormented by want.

O when shall these evils come to an end? When shall I be free of the terrible bondage of my sins? When, O Lord, shall I hold you alone in my mind? When shall I rejoice fully in you? When shall I be entirely free of all obstacles to true liberty, all troubles of mind and body? When shall I be wholly at peace—a peace that is stable and unchanging, an interior and exterior peace, a peace completely assured?

O merciful Jesus, when shall I stand and behold you, and contemplate the glory of your Kingdom? When will you be all in all to me? When shall I be with you in your Kingdom, which you had prepared, from all eternity, for those who love you?

Here am I, a poor, banished creature in the land of my enemies, where wars and terrible calamities encompass me daily. Comfort me in my banishment, Lord, and soothe my sorrow. All my desire longs for you. Everything in this life is a burden to me, despite what this world offers by way of consolation. I long to enjoy you inwardly but am unable to do so.

It is my desire to devote myself completely to heavenly things; but worldly concerns and unsubdued passions continue to drag me down. My spirit desires to rise above all material things; but my flesh keeps me, against my will, subject to them. Unhappy as I am, I therefore fight against myself and become a cause of grief to myself; for my spirit seeks to carry me up, but my flesh, to drag me down.

Whenever my mind turns to heavenly things, and when I pray, I suffer inwardly because a rush of carnal temptations and thoughts distracts me. O God, be not far from me! Do not turn in anger from your servant. Let fly your arrows and rout the promptings of the Enemy; with your lightning, scatter the forces of evil. Gather in my senses to you; call them home; help me to set aside all worldly cares; show me how to banish and scorn all vicious thoughts.

O everlasting Truth, assist me, so that nothing vain

may move me. Come to me, O heavenly Sweetness, and scatter all unholiness from your sight. Give me your pardon, and deal mercifully with me whenever, during prayer, my thoughts wander from you. Indeed, I must confess that I am easy prey to distractions. Over and over again it happens that I am not where my body is sitting or standing, but wherever my thoughts have taken me. Where my thoughts are, there also am I; and all too often, where my thoughts are, there lie my interests too. Whatever I have found pleasant or learned to enjoy, that is the distraction most likely to capture my attention.

It is as you have truly said (you who are Truth itself): "Where your treasure is, there your heart is also" (Matthew 6.21). If I love Heaven, I willingly give thought to things of Heaven. If I love the world, I rejoice in any happiness the world provides me and grieve over the pain it causes me. If I love the flesh, my mind is constantly addicted to what pleases the flesh. If I love the soul, I enjoy taking an interest in the spiritual life. Whatever it is I love, that is what I enjoy hearing and speaking of; and that is what I assimilate into my life.

But blessed is the person who, for your sake, O Lord, is willing to live detached from created goods, who deals violently with his natural self, and whose devoutness of soul crucifies the appetites of the body—so that he may offer you holy prayers with a quiet conscience and, having excluded worldly things from both his inner and his outer life, be judged worthy to be admitted into the choirs of angels.

xlix. *Turn your longings toward life everlasting, for the rewards promised to faithful souls are great.*

THE VOICE OF CHRIST:

At those moments, my child, when you feel a desire for unending happiness to be poured out upon you from above, and for release from the tabernacle of your body so that you may witness my glory unchanging, open wide your heart and give a warm welcome to that holy inspiration. Offer thanks to the Goodness of Heaven, who treats you so courteously, visits you so mercifully, stirs you so fervently, comforts you so effectively, keeping you from sinking of your own weight back to earthly concerns.

You cannot obtain such a favor by your own efforts or planning, but only through God's free grace and interest in your welfare, with this purpose: that you may make progress in virtue and deep humility, preparing yourself for the difficulties that will come, bending your will to seek after me with all your heart's affection and to serve me with a devout willingness.

As you know, my child, when a fire is burning, it often happens that the flames leap up along with smoke. Likewise, what some persons desire is to rise toward heavenly things even though they are not entirely free of the smoke of fleshly temptations. It is therefore not entirely for the purpose of giving honor to God that they send him their petitions. Your own desires are often of that kind, though you profess them to be serious and sincere. Any of your desires that are tainted by self-interest and concern for your own advantage cannot be called pure or perfect.

Do not ask for what you would find profitable and pleasant to receive, but for what is acceptable to me and will give me honor. If your judgment is sound, you will prefer and follow what I desire for you, rather than your own preference or any particular thing you might desire. For I already know what you desire; I have often heard your longings. Already you long to enjoy the glorious liberty of the children of God. Already you desire the delights of your everlasting home, your joyful heavenly abode. But your hour has not yet come. You have yet another hour, a period of conflict, work, and trial. You desire to be filled with the Greatest Good; but, for the present, you cannot attain your goal. I am the One you long for. Wait for me till the Kingdom of God arrives.

Here on earth, you are to receive further trials and be anxious about many things. Sometimes, you will receive spiritual comforting, but not equal to your desire. Be brave, therefore, and steel yourself to do and suffer things you would naturally prefer to avoid. You have an obligation to put on the new man and to make yourself into a new person. You have an obligation also to do things you would prefer not to do, and to leave undone many things you would like to do. You will see others enjoying success with their plans while your plans fail. You will see others listened to when they speak while your words are ignored. What others ask for, they will receive; you also will ask but will not receive. Others will be praised by many, but nothing in your favor will be said of you. Others will be entrusted with various responsibilities while you will be treated as of no use. On such occasions, you will naturally feel slighted; and it will be to your benefit to endure your slights in silence. The Lord's faithful servants can expect to be tried often in such ways, which test their ability to deny themselves and break their own willfulness in all things.

The most important way in which you need to learn to die to yourself is by recognizing and enduring things that you would rather avoid, especially when you are commanded to do something that you consider an imposition or not worth doing. It is only because you are under another's authority that you find it hard to be at another's beck and call and to set aside your own preferences.

But if you look ahead to the fruit of your labors, my child, you will see that the end is near at hand and the reward beyond compare. Then you will not find it so hard to bear your burdens but will be borne up strongly by your own patience. If you can give up readily your desire to have your own way in small things now, you will find that you will always have what you desire in Heaven. There you will certainly find everything you may desire, everything you *could* desire. There, within your reach, you will have every good thing without fear of losing it. There too, your will and mine will be as one; you will be free from all desire to have any good, visible or invisible, that belongs to another. No one will cross you there; no one will oppose you, and nothing will stand in your way; your every desire will be satisfied, your every longing refreshed and filled, as if to the brim. In return for the neglect you suffer now, I shall give you a share in my own glory; your heaviness of heart will be clothed in a garment of praise; and your low estate will be exchanged for a kingly throne forever. There in Heaven, you will see the fruits of your obedience; your works of repentance will bring you rejoicing, and your humbleness of service will receive a glorious crown.

For the present, therefore, be humble and bend yourself to all necessity, without asking who said this or commanded that. If your superior, or even an equal or a subordinate, makes a request of your assistance or even indirectly seeks it, let it be your special care to cooperate with a good will and make a sincere effort to do what is asked of you. Let this person ask this of you, and that person something else; let this person be praised for one thing, and that person for another, even a thousand thousand times. Do not look for excuses to praise yourself for this or that, but hold yourself in contempt and rejoice only in doing whatever gives good pleasure and honor to me. This should be your whole desire, so that in your life and in your death, God may always be glorified through you.

1. *When you are downcast, place yourself in God's care.*
THE DISCIPLE:
O Lord God, heavenly Father: blessed be you now and forever. As you decree, so does it happen. And all that you do is good. Allow your servant to rejoice in you,

rather than in myself or any other thing. You alone are my true gladness.

You, O Lord, are my hope and my crown, my joy and my honor. What can I call mine that I have not received from you, even without having deserved anything? All that exists—what you have made and what you have given—belongs to you.

From my earliest years, I have known want and trouble. At times, my soul is sad even to the point of tears. Other times, my spirit is disturbed at the thought of impending sufferings. I long for the joy that comes with your peace. I seek the peace that you promised your children, whom you feed with your comforting enlightenment. If you should grant me your peace and fill me with your holy joy, my soul would be full of music and sing devoutly your praise.

But if you should withdraw yourself from me—as oftentimes you do—your servant would be unable to keep to the path marked out by your commandments. He would fall on his knees and strike his breast, complaining that the time of your favors had passed, when your candle gave light to his mind and your wing gave him protection from the temptations besetting him.

O just and ever-praiseworthy Father, now comes the hour when your servant is to be tested. Yet it is right, beloved Father, that your servant suffer awhile for your sake at this time. My ever-honored Father, this is the hour that you knew from all eternity would come to me: the brief hour when your servant must outwardly be oppressed while inwardly living faithful to you! This is the hour when I must be for a short while despised and disgraced, when I shall fail in the eyes of others and be brought low by sadness and heaviness of heart. But all this I welcome, so that I may rise again with you in the dawning of your new Light and be glorified with you in Heaven. Holy Father, this is the way you have appointed and willed for me. And what you have commanded is what must take place.

Truly *this hour* is a favor you give to your friends, that they should accept their suffering out of love for you and be assaulted in this world, no matter how often, no matter by whom, no matter what the circumstances, according to your will. On this earth, nothing happens without the approval of your counsel and providence.

Lord, it is good that you have humbled me, so that I might learn the justness of your judgments and abandon all pride of heart and presumption. It is a profit to me that shame has covered my face, so that I might learn to seek comfort from you rather than from others. You have taught me to fear your unsearchable judgments, for I have seen that you send affliction to both the holy and the wicked but treat all with equity and justice.

Therefore I give you thanks, O Lord, that you have not spared my sins, but have worn down my willfulness with hard lashes, inflicting me with sorrow, sending me anxieties within and without. Under Heaven, Lord, there is no one else who can comfort me, only you, my God. You are the Divine Physician of souls, which you heal by buffeting; you take them through Hell and back again. Let your discipline govern me; your rod will teach me.

O beloved Father, look on me and see that I bow myself to the rod of your correction. Strike my back and neck, and make me bend my crookedness into the shape you desire. Make of me a conscientious, humble servant, in your kindness, so that whenever you beckon, I shall be ready to command. I place myself and all that is mine in your care, to be corrected. I would much rather be punished in this life than hereafter.

All things, in whole and in their parts, you know; and nothing in anyone's conscience is hidden from you. Before anything is done, you knew that it would be done. You have no need for anyone to teach or correct you concerning what happens here on earth. You know what is best for my spiritual growth—and also how well the rust of my sinfulness is scraped off by my suffering. Deal with me, therefore, in any way that suits your good pleasure. Do not turn away from me because of my sinful life (the details of which you know most thoroughly).

O Lord, I pray that I may know what is worth knowing, love what is worth loving, praise whatever pleases you most, esteem what is most precious to you, and shun whatever is filthy or unclean in your sight. Keep me from judging on the basis of what my bodily eyes can see; and from giving credence to what my ears hear from the mouths of the ignorant. But lead me instead to true judgment of things material and spiritual; above all, to search constantly to know the good pleasure of your will for me.

Our minds are often deceived in their judgments. Many persons are self-deceived and love only what their eyes can see. And in what way is anyone better off for having won the esteem of flatterers? They only shame themselves who flatter the poser, praise the fool, honor the self-appointed seer, or puff up the merits of slackers.

It is as the humble Saint Francis said: what a person is in your sight, that he is, and nothing more.

li. *At the very least, make yourself available for humble service.*

THE VOICE OF CHRIST:

My child, you are not always able to keep yourself full of desire for what is virtuous, nor to maintain the higher pitch of contemplation. Because of the weakness of your nature, you cannot but fall to a lower level and bear the wearying burden of a corruptible life, despite your efforts to escape it. So long as you carry with you a mortal body, weariness and heaviness of heart will be your lot. You do well, therefore, while you are in the flesh, to complain of its burdens, which prevent your devoting yourself steadfastly to spiritual learning and divine contemplation.

Thus it is that you are well advised to give yourself humbly to exterior works of charity, refreshing your spirit by doing them; to look forward with confidence to my coming and to Heaven's visitation; to endure your state of banishment and your spiritual dryness patiently till I next come to you and relieve your anxieties. I shall make you forget your sorrows and troubles and teach you to enjoy a complete inner stillness. I shall spread out before you the pleasant fields of the Scriptures, so that, with a larger heart, you can set out to hurry along the path marked by my commandments.

Then you will say, "The present sufferings are as nothing compared to the glory that will be revealed to us" (Romans 8.18).

lii. *Think of yourself as more deserving to be punished than to be commended.*

THE DISCIPLE:

Lord, I deserve neither your consolation nor your spiritual visitations. When you leave me poor and isolated, you deal justly with me. Even if I were to shed a sea of tears, I would not merit your comfortings. The only thing I do deserve is to be scourged and punished, because of my many grave sins and my frequent and grievous offences toward you. So it is that truth and reason are best satisfied in judging me unworthy of the least comfort.

Yet it is not your will, O gracious and merciful God, that any of your works should perish, but instead that your mercies be vessels carrying signs of your bountiful goodness. It is your own choice to comfort your servant beyond any deserving, beyond what any human being could merit. For your consolations cannot be compared to any comfort that lies in human words.

For what reason, O Lord, have you bestowed any comfort on me? I cannot remember any good I have done, but only that I have been ever tending toward sin and slow to amend. This truth I cannot deny. Were I to claim otherwise, you would give testimony against me and none would come forward to defend me. What have I merited by my sins except the everlasting fires of Hell? I confess and acknowledge that I deserve only scorn and contempt. I am unworthy to be numbered among your devout servants. And though my ears would rather not hear it, I shall nevertheless testify against myself and confess my sins so that I might be found worthy of your mercy.

What should I say beyond this: that I am guilty and full of contradictions. I can bring myself to say only this: "I have sinned, O Lord, I have sinned! Have mercy and pardon me."

Be patient with me and grant me this brief time to repent my sins, before I pass through the land of darkness, the land that lies beneath the shadow of Death. For you desire of the miserable, guilty sinner only that he be contrite and do penance humbly for his sins.

A hope for your forgiveness is born of sincere contrition and humility of heart. Thus is the troubled conscience reconciled with itself; thus is recovered the grace lost to sin; thus is one preserved from your anger on the Last Day; and thus do God and the penitent soul meet with a joyful kiss.

The same humble contrition is a sacrifice acceptable to you, O Lord, its fragrance more agreeable to you than the perfume of incense. Or it is the sweet ointment to be poured over your sacred feet. For you have never despised a humble and contrite heart.

In contrition we find refuge from the angry face of Satan; thereby too we restore and cleanse what was defiled and polluted elsewhere.

liii. *By cultivating your appetite for material things, you prevent the grace of God from coming to you.*

THE VOICE OF CHRIST:

Consider, my child, how precious my grace is—so much so that it cannot be combined with earthly comforts and material things. You ought to look for ways to cast aside everything that hinders your reception of grace, if you desire to have it. Find for yourself a place apart; learn to love being alone with yourself, having no desire for conversation there, rather offering devout prayer to God. Thus you may keep your mind composed and your conscience clear. Hold the world as nothing; prefer to place yourself in God's service than to busy yourself with outward affairs. You will be unable to give your attention to me if you take delight in transient business. You are well advised to keep yourself detached even from your acquaintances and close friends and to free your mind from all worldly comforts.

The saintly Apostle Peter rightly urged that the followers of Christ regard themselves as pilgrim-strangers in this world (1 Peter 2.11).

At the hour of death, how confident will be the person who is free of any undue attachment to anything of this world. The sickly soul does not understand the benefit of having a heart free from attachment to material things; just as the libertine does not understand the liberty of the holy person. Anyone who would be truly holy should detach himself from both distant and close relationships and beware mostly of himself. If you can perfectly overcome your natural self, you will find it very easy to govern every other aspect of your life. To triumph over oneself is the perfect victory.

The one who can subject himself to the point where his sense-driven appetites remain obedient to reason and his reason is obedient to me—he is the one who is truly called conqueror (of himself) and lord (of the world).

If you aspire to that high goal, set out courageously and lay ax to the root: that is, the root of selfishness. Then you will be able to pull up and destroy your inner tendency toward selfishness and your lust for every personal and earthly good. It is precisely your vicious tendency to love yourself excessively that leaves ungoverned almost everything that ought to be brought under control and subjection. If you could but once vanquish and subdue this evil, you would find that a great peace and tranquillity would follow.

Because so few strive to become perfectly dead to

themselves or to detach themselves from their selfish bent, they live wrapped up in the net of their self-interests, and their souls cannot find a way to rise above themselves. Anyone who desires to walk freely with me must learn to mortify all evil and spurious cravings and leave off every selfish affection for any created thing.

liv. *A truly spiritual person has learned to distinguish the promptings of Nature from those of Grace.*

THE VOICE OF CHRIST:

Pay careful attention, my child, to the difference between the promptings of Nature and those of Grace. They work in ways that are hard to distinguish but are actually contrary to each other; and only a spiritually enlightened person can tell them apart.

All human persons desire what is good and pretend there is something good in all their words and deeds. Many are deceived by the outward appearance of goodness. Nature is a crafty seducer of many; she deceives and entraps them, and has only one purpose and goal to serve—herself. Grace, on the other hand, carries herself modestly, avoids everything that is evil, never works under cover of false pretenses, and acts always and entirely for God's sake, in whom she resides.

Nature, again, fights against death, against being subjected or kept down, against being overcome, and is not easily controlled. But Grace looks for opportunities for self-mortification, resists sensuality, desires to be in servitude and even to be defeated, and has no wish to take advantage of her own liberty. She is happiest when kept under discipline. She does not seek to hold power over anyone, being content to live, remain, and subsist under God's providence, ready to cooperate with every human ordinance.

Nature works for her own advantage and looks for opportunities to use another for her own profit. Grace is uninterested in what is "profitable" or advantageous to herself, but seeks only the good of others. Nature enjoys having herself honored and reverenced, but Grace assigns all honor and glory to God. Nature shuns anything that might bring her shame or contempt, whereas Grace happily suffers ignominy for Jesus' name. Nature enjoys leisure and bodily comfort. Grace cannot bear to be unoccupied and accepts every task cheerfully.

Nature tries to acquire beautiful and rare things and has nothing to do with anything crude or ugly. Grace finds delight in the humble and the plain, does not despise unpolished things, and does not refuse to wear what is old and mended. Nature values temporal things, rejoices at earthly gains, is saddened by material losses, and is irritated by the smallest word of censure. Grace, however, values what is eternal, has no attachment to temporal things, is undisturbed at any loss thereof, and is not soured by hard words—because her treasure and joy are in Heaven, where nothing perishes.

Nature is also covetous. She would rather receive than give and takes special pleasure in having things she can hold as her very own. But Grace is kind-hearted and generous. She is free of any private interests, is contented with a little, and considers it more blessed to give than to receive.

Nature leads a person to an attachment to other creatures, to his own body, to foolish longings, and to a hundred different fads and fancies. Grace instead draws close to God and every virtue, renounces every attachment to material things, avoids the world, hates the unregulated desires of the flesh, restricts herself from aimless wandering, and even blushes to be seen in public. Nature gladly accepts any external comforts, especially those that delight the senses. Grace finds consolation in God alone and delights in the highest Good rather than in any visible things.

Nature strives to turn everything to her own advantage and profit. She cannot bring herself to do anything without thought of repayment. She expects her every kindness to be returned in equal measure, or better, or at least in the form of praise. For she is eager to have her works and gifts and words highly valued. Grace, on the contrary, has no temporal goals and desires no other reward than God; nor does she expect more of temporal necessities than that they help her obtain eternal benefits.

Nature rejoices at her many friends and relatives, prides herself on her noble status and birth, smiles on the powerful, dotes on the wealthy, and applauds any who resemble herself. But Grace loves even her enemies and does not long to be adulated by any large number of friends. She sees nothing of value in high birth unless it be combined with the much more valuable thing—virtue. She favors the poor rather than the rich, has more sympathy with the innocent than with the powerful, rejoices with the person of integrity rather than one whose life is deceitful. She never ceases to urge good persons to strive for the highest rewards and, in all the ways of virtue, imitate Christ, the Son of God.

Nature is quick to complain at any threat of trouble or deprivation. Grace remains firm and constant when difficulty must be endured. Nature judges all things in relation to herself and works and argues on her own behalf. But Grace returns everything to God, from whom all things come. She disclaims any goodness in herself and is not given to arrogance. She keeps herself free of contention and does not use her opinion as a weapon against others. In everything concerning the senses and the intellect, she submits to the eternal Wisdom and Judge.

Nature is anxious to know secrets, to hear the latest news. She likes to parade herself in public and to trust her own senses for judging the truth of things. It is her desire that she be fully acknowledged, and she enjoys doing anything that will bring herself praise and admiration. But Grace is uninterested in "news," and is not given to curiosity about this and that (for such curiosity is a side-effect of the original corruption of human nature); in her eyes, there is nothing new, or even lasting, on earth. Hence Grace teaches the restraint of the senses, the avoidance of smugness and showiness, the humility of hiding whatever others might admire or praise, the seeking for truly nourishing fruit from all matter and knowledge, and the praising and honoring of God. She does not permit herself or anything that belongs to her to be praised publicly. Her desire is that God, who out of sheer love caused all things to exist, be blessed in his gifts.

This "grace" is a supernatural light, a specific and special gift of God. It is also a distinguishing mark of the elect and a pledge of everlasting salvation. It lifts a person up from earthly concerns so that the things of Heaven can be loved. It changes a person from carnal to spiritual.

Hence it follows that the more one subdues and brings under control the natural self, the greater the grace that can be infused. Thus, each day, through new infusions of grace, the inner person is reformed in closer accord with the image of God.

lv. *Because our human nature is fallen and corrupted by sin, we depend on the healing and strengthening that only divine grace can supply.*

THE DISCIPLE:

O Lord God, after your own image and likeness you created me. Grant me this grace which you have shown me is so powerful and necessary for my salvation. Grant that I may subdue my evil-prone nature, which tugs me toward sin, and thus toward damnation. I can feel in my flesh "the law of sin contradicting the law of my mind" (Romans 7.23). The law of sin leads me toward slavery—slavery to the senses—in many ways. I am unable to resist my own passions unless your most holy grace be firmly established in my heart and assists me.

My need for your grace, even for abundant grace, arises from my desire to overcome my own nature—a nature that has been prone to evil from its early days. For it is through the first man, Adam, that human nature was weakened and corrupted by sin; and the penalty of this fault has descended on all humanity. The result is that the entire order of nature, which you created good and upright, has come to be a symbol of the vice and weakness of corrupted human nature; for when left to itself, it tends toward evil and base things. The little strength remaining in human nature is like a spark lying hidden among ashes. That spark is natural reason, which, surrounded by the darkness of ignorance, is yet able to tell the difference between good and evil, between truth and falsity. Nevertheless, it is unable to fulfill all that it approves, and it does not enjoy the full light of the truth or of sound judgment.

Hence it is, O God, that I take delight in your law for the sake of the inner man, knowing your commandments to be good and just and holy, confirming as they do the necessity to avoid all evil and sin. But I, in the flesh, still serve the law of sin, obeying my sense appetites rather than my reason. Thus it happens that, though I desire to do what is good, I do not know how to do it. Hence too, though I often begin with good intentions, I soon grow slack and give up because my weakness lacks the assistance of your grace. So it happens that I know the way of perfection and see clearly how I *should* act. But, under the influence of my own sinfulness, I fail to rise to a more holy level.

O Lord, how necessary your grace is to me—for the beginning of anything good, for persevering with it, and for accomplishing it! Without your grace, I can do nothing; but when your grace strengthens me, I can do all things in you. O truly heavenly grace, without which my most worthy acts are as nothing, and my natural gifts are worthless! Apart from your grace, O Lord, all arts, riches, beauty, strength, wit, and eloquence are of no value in your sight. Such natural gifts are possessed by both good and evil persons. It is the special gift of the elect that they possess your grace and love. Those who bear this sign are accounted worthy of eternal life. So valuable is this grace that the gift of prophecy, or of working of miracles, or of intellectual insight, is worthless without it. Apart from charity and grace, not even faith, hope, or any other virtue is acceptable to you.

How blessed is that grace, which makes the poor in spirit rich in virtues, and which makes one who is rich in material possessions humble of heart!

Come, Lord, come unto me; come and replenish me soon with your comforting grace, for otherwise my soul will faint from weariness and my spirit will wither away. Lord, I ask that I might find grace in your sight. Your grace is sufficient for me, even though nothing else that my nature longs for is obtained. As long as your grace is with me, I shall fear no evils, though I be tempted and annoyed by many grievances. In it alone is my strength; through it alone do I receive your help and guidance. For it is stronger than any enemy and wiser than any seer.

Your grace, dear Lord, is the mistress of truth, the teacher of self-discipline, the light of the heart, the comfort of the sorrowing, the nurse of devotion, the chaser of fear, and the fountain-source of tears. Without it, what am I but brittle wood, a dead branch, fit only to be discarded?

Therefore, O Lord, let your grace go before me and follow me, inspiring me to give myself continuously to good works. This I ask through your Son, Jesus Christ. Amen.

lvi. *If you would learn to imitate Christ, even to accepting the cross, learn to deny yourself.*

THE VOICE OF CHRIST:

The more you succeed in drawing yourself away from self-serving, the more closely will you approach me. Just as the way to achieve an inner peace is to abandon all your desires for external goods, so too the way to unite yourself with God is to abandon all your inner selfishness. I wish you to learn to resign yourself perfectly to my will, without complaint or indecision.

Follow after me. "I am the way, the truth, and the life" (John 14.6). Apart from the Way, you make no progress. Apart from the Truth, there is no knowing. And apart from the Life, there is no living. I am the Way you must follow, the Truth in whom you must trust, and the Life you ought to hope for. I am the safe

Way, the unerring Truth, and the endless Life. I am the straightest Way, the highest Truth, and the authentic blessed and uncreated Life. If you keep yourself on my Way, you will come to know my Truth. My Truth will make you free, and you will take possession of eternal life.

If you desire to enter into that life, keep the commandments. If you desire to know what is true, place your faith in me. If you wish to be perfect, sell all your belongings. If you desire to be my disciple, deny yourself completely. If you wish to possess a blessed life, hold your present life in no esteem. If you would like to be exalted in Heaven, bear yourself with humility in this world. If you desire to reign with me, carry my cross with me. Only those who are "servants of the cross" will find the way of blessedness and true enlightenment.

THE DISCIPLE:

Lord Jesus, because your Way is narrow and despised by the world, grant me the grace to imitate you even though the world will hold me in contempt for doing so. For the servant is no greater than his lord, nor is the disciple above his master. Train your servant in your way of life; that is, the way of salvation and true holiness. For I have found that merely reading or hearing about it brings me less than complete satisfaction or happiness.

THE VOICE OF CHRIST:

My child, now that you have read and learned much about it, you will find happiness if you put it into practice. "The one who hears my commandments and keeps them is the one who loves me; and I shall love him and reveal myself to him" (John 14.21). And I shall see that he sits beside me in my Father's Kingdom.

THE DISCIPLE:

Lord Jesus, what you have said and promised will truly come to pass; and I pray that I may not be wholly unworthy of this favor. I have received the cross, received it from your own hand. I shall bear it, even till death, because you have asked me to carry it. In truth, the life of a faithful Christian is a cross—yet it is also a guide to paradise. Having now begun, it is not lawful that I turn back or abandon what I have undertaken.

—Dear friends in Christ, let all of us take courage and go forward together, knowing that Jesus will be with us. We have taken up the cross for Jesus' sake; let us persevere in carrying it for his sake. He will be our helper, guide, and scout. See how our King leads us on, ready to do battle for us. Let us follow him bravely. Let none of us fear any terror. Let all of us be prepared to die valiantly in the battle and keep our glory unstained by any cowardly fleeing from the cross.

lvii. Do not allow your own imperfections to cause you to lose hope.

THE VOICE OF CHRIST:

My child, your patience and humility in the face of trials please me more than your contentment and devotion when all is well with you. Why should you allow every little complaint aimed at you to cause you grief?

Even if you had to bear up under much worse, you ought not let it disturb you. Let it pass. It is not the first such thing that has happened to you, nor is there anything new in it; and if you live longer, it will not be the last. It seems you are courageous enough so long as nothing comes along to test you! It seems too that you are able to offer a word of good counsel and encouragement to others, but lose your own strength and good judgment as soon as you find yourself in difficulty.

Take note, then, of the many little things that have caused you to experience your own weakness. Such things happen to you, nevertheless, for your own good.

As much as you can, keep yourself from nursing a past grievance in your heart; and when a trial falls on you, do not let it cast you down or long bother you. If you find it hard to bear up joyfully, be patient at least.

Though you dislike to hear a word said against you, and it makes you indignant, put a restraint on yourself and allow no word of anger to escape your lips lest you give scandal to Christ's little ones. The present storm will soon pass into calm, and your grief of soul will be soothed by the return of grace. "I still live," says your Lord, "and am ready to help you and give you ever more consolation if you but trust in me and call devoutly for my assistance."

Be more patient of soul; prepare yourself for greater trials. If you find yourself often scorned or strongly tempted, all is not lost. You are a human creature, not God; you are in the flesh, not an angel. How can you expect to continue in the same virtuous state when an angel in Heaven and the first man in the Garden of Paradise both fell from grace. I am the One who lifts up the dejected to a place of safety and wholeness. And I advance those who admit their own weakness to a share in my divinity.

THE DISCIPLE:

Lord, blessed is your word, more sweet to my taste than honey and the honeycomb. What would I do in all my difficulties and anxiety if you did not comfort me with your holy counseling? Why should I be so concerned about what and how much I suffer if I am eventually to reach the port of salvation? Grant me the grace of a good death and a fair passage out of this world. Remember me, O Lord, and guide me in the Way that leads directly to your Kingdom. Amen.

lviii. *Do not try to understand the mysterious ways of God.*

THE VOICE OF CHRIST:

My child, be sure to keep yourself from getting into disputes about deep questions and the hidden judgments of God—about why this person was so highly favored while that person was so grievously afflicted and still another person was so swiftly promoted. Such matters are beyond human understanding; and neither reason nor argument can search out the judgments of God. So when Satan tempts you to get involved in such questions, or when others raise a question out of curiosity, make the prophet's answer your own: "You are just, O Lord, and your judgment is right" (Psalm 119.137).

And again: "The judgments of the Lord are entirely true and justified" (Psalm 19.9).

My judgments are to be feared, not made the topic for discussion; for they are beyond the power of the human mind to understand.

So too, I caution you against getting into a discussion or argument about the relative merits of saintly persons—as to which of them is holier, or which will have the higher place in Heaven. Such debates often lead to useless strife and bitterness. They also breed pride and haughtiness of mind, which are themselves the source of envy and dissension—as one person promotes the merits of one saint while another favors some other saint. There is no good end served by such squabbling; rather it displeases the saints themselves. I am not the God of discord, but of peace; and my peace rests on humility, not self-display.

Some are carried away by their enthusiasm for one or another group of saints; but this enthusiasm is a human, rather than a divine, sort of love. I am he who made all the saints; I, who gave them grace; and I, who brought them to glory. I know what each has deserved; I have led them along with the blessings of my own goodness. Before the world began, I knew who my beloved ones would be. I chose them out of the world; they did not first choose me. With my grace, I called them; with my mercy, I drew them. And I led them safely through all kinds of temptations. I poured wonderful consolations into them, gave them the gift of perseverance, and crowned their patience.

From the first to the last, I acknowledge them and embrace them all with immeasurable love. It is I who am to be praised in my saints; it is I who am to be blessed above all persons and things; and it is I who am to be honored in all those persons whom I have lifted up to predestined glory without their having any antecedent merits of their own.

Hence anyone who despises even the least of those who belong to me give no honor to the greatest; for I have made both the great and the small. And anyone who speaks ill of any of the saints, speaks ill also of me and of all the others in the kingdom of Heaven. For all the saints are as one, united by the bond of charity; in one thought and will and love, they are united one with another.

Of course—and what is more important—their love for me is stronger than their love for themselves or for their accomplishments. Being entirely free of self-love and rapt beyond themselves, they are completely moved to love me, in whom they have their fully satisfying rest. Nothing can turn them away or depress them. Full of the everlasting Truth, they burn with an unquenchable flame of charity.

So let all flesh-bound and "natural" persons, those who cannot "love" anything except what brings them pleasure, give up their disputing about the conditions of the saints of God. Such persons give pluses and minuses according to their own fancies rather than depend on what is actually pleasing to eternal Truth.

Many persons, especially those who are little informed, cannot love with a perfect, spiritual sort of love because of their ignorance. They are still so much under the influence of their natural affections and their friendship with this or that person, that they base their ideas about heavenly things on their own experience of human endearments. There is a radical difference between what their weak imaginations can envision and what enlightened minds can "see," thanks to the revelation the latter receive from above.

Be cautious, therefore, my child. Do not let vain curiosity lead you to concern yourself with matters beyond your knowing. Instead, let it be your chief business and effort to obtain a place in the Kingdom of God, even if it is only the lowest place.

Suppose there were a person who knew which saints had a higher rank or which could be said to excel in sanctity in the kingdom of Heaven: what profit would there be in such knowledge if that person were not humble in my sight and did not rise to offer the greatest praise to my name as a consequence of having that knowledge? The person who reflects on the gravity of his own sins and the poverty of his virtues is far more pleasing to God (even though he or she is far from equaling the perfection of the saints) than one who gets involved in disputes about who is "major" and who is "minor."

The saints themselves would be quite contented if you on earth would show as much contentment and leave off from your vain quarreling. They certainly do not glory in their own merits, for they claim to have no goodness of themselves, and credit everything to me; for it was my limitless love that provided them with everything. Their own love for God so fills them with an overflowing joy that none of them lacks anything in glory or happiness. With all the saints, the more humble they are in themselves, the greater their glory and the nearer and dearer they are to me. Hence it is that it was written, "They cast down their crowns before God and fell on their faces before the Lamb, and adored him who lives forever and ever" (Revelation 4.10).

Many of those who concern themselves about who is the greatest in the Kingdom of God don't even know whether they themselves will be numbered among the least there. In Heaven, where all are "great," it is a great thing to be the very least. For there all are called, and in fact are, "Sons of God." Thus it is written: "the least will be the equivalent of a thousand" (Isaiah 60.22) and "the hundred-year-old sinner will die" (65.20). When the disciples asked Jesus who would be the greatest in the kingdom of Heaven, the answer they received was simply this: "Unless you become again as small children, you will not enter the kingdom of Heaven; whosoever will humble himself like this little child, that is the one who will be greatest in the kingdom of Heaven" (Matthew 18.3).

Woe to those who decline to humble themselves willingly in the manner of little children: the low gate of the kingdom of Heaven will not allow them to enter. Woe also to the wealthy, who have their comforts in this world; while the poor enter the Kingdom of God, *they* will be left standing outside, lamenting.

You who are humble: rejoice. You who are poor: be filled with joy. If only you walk the way of Truth, yours is the Kingdom of God.

lix. *Place all your hope and trust in God alone.*
THE DISCIPLE:
Lord, in this life, in what can I place my confidence, and where can I find the most comfort in anything under Heaven? Is the answer not you, O Lord God, whose mercies are without number? When have I ever been well except when you were with me? And how could I be ill when you were present to me? I would much rather be poor and have you than be rich and find you absent. I would rather be a pilgrim on earth accompanied by you than possess Heaven and not have you there. Wherever you are, there is my Heaven; where you are not, there Death and Hell reside. Because you are all my desire, I have no choice but to sigh and call and pray earnestly to you. The truth is, there is no one whom I can entirely trust, no one able to help me promptly in my times of need, except you, my God. You are my hope; you are my comforter, most faithful to me through thick and thin.

Every person seeks what is advantageous to himself; you alone have concerned yourself with *my* salvation and profit and turn everything to my advantage. Though you allow me to be beset by temptations and troubles, yet you have ordered even these for my benefit, for it is your custom to test those whom you love in a thousand ways. When you put me to a trial, you deserve no less of my love and praise than I would give you if I were full of heavenly consolations.

In you, Lord God, I therefore place all my hope and seek all my refuge. I rest all my trials and anxieties upon you, for I find that I am weak and unreliable concerning anything I try to handle apart from you. My many friends cannot assist me, strong arms cannot help me, experienced experts cannot advise me, the books of scholars cannot comfort me, expensive potions cannot heal me, and no place, be it ever so secluded and beautiful, can shelter me—unless you yourself assist, help, instruct, strengthen, console, and shelter me.

All the many material things that seem to offer the promise of peace and happiness are of no effect apart from you, and, in fact, bring no happiness at all. You are the fountain of all that is good; you are the height of life and the depth of what could be spoken. What brings most comfort to your servants is to place their hope above all else in you.

To you, therefore, I lift up my eyes. In you, O God, the Father of Mercies, I put my confidence. With your heavenly blessings, sanctify my soul. Make her suitable to be your holy dwelling and the center of your eternal glory. Let nothing that might offend the eyes of your majesty be found in this temple of your divinity.

Look upon me with your customary goodness and your abundant mercies, and hear the prayers of your lowly servant, who lives far exiled from you in this land, under the shadow of death. Protect and preserve the soul of this, the least of your servants, living among the many dangers of this mortal life. Send your grace to accompany me, directing my soul along the way of peace, toward her home of unending brightness. Amen.

Book Four

The Imitation of Christ

On the Blessed Sacrament

Come to me, all you who labor and are heavily burdened, and I shall refresh you. — Matthew 11.28

The Bread that I shall give is my flesh, for the life of the world. — John 6.52

Take and eat: this is my body, which will be given up for you. Do this in memory of me.
— 1 Corinthians 11.24

He who eats my flesh and drinks my blood abides in me, and I in him. — John 6.57

The words I have spoken to you are spirit and life.
— John 6.64

i. *Receive Christ with the greatest reverence.*

THE DISCIPLE:

Those words, O Christ, are yours, the everlasting Truth; though they were not all spoken on a single occasion or written in one place. Because they are your words, and therefore true, they are words I must thankfully and prayerfully accept. They are yours, for you have spoken them; but they are mine also, for you spoke them on behalf of my salvation. I accept them cheerfully from your mouth in order to plant them deeply in my heart.

Your words—most gracious and abounding in love —stir my heart. But my own sins discourage me, and my wayward conscience keeps me from welcoming such great mysteries. The kindness in your words brings me encouragement, but my many sins drag me down.

You command me to come to you with confidence if I would have a share of your life; and to receive the food of everlasting life if I would obtain unending life and glory. "Come unto me," you have said, "all you who labor and are burdened, and I shall refresh you." How sweet and loving are your words in the sinner's ears, my Lord God, you who invite the poor and the needy to share in your own most holy body and blood.

But who am I, Lord, that I should presume to approach you? Behold: the highest Heaven cannot contain you and yet you say, "Come, all of you, to me." What can be the meaning of so gracious and so loving an invitation? How shall I—who can see no good in myself on which to presume—dare to accept it? How can I, who have so often offended you in your most gentle sight, bring you "into my house"?

Angels and archangels stand in awe of you; righteous and holy persons fear you; and still you say, "Come, all of you, to me." If you did not say so, Lord, who would believe it could be so? And if you had not made it a command, who would try to draw near you?

Did not Noah, a most just man, labor a hundred years in constructing an ark in order that he and a few others might be saved? And how can I, in a single hour, prepare myself to receive, with reverence, the Maker of the world?

Your great servant and special friend Moses likewise made an ark of the finest wood and covered it over with a layer of purest gold, as a place wherein to keep the tablets of your law. How then shall I, a flawed creature, presume so casually to receive the Maker of the law and the Giver of life?

Solomon too, the wisest of the kings of Israel, devoted seven years to the construction of a magnificent temple in praise of your name; and then, during the eight-day celebration at its dedication, he sacrificed to you a thousand peace-offerings and, amid the sound of trumpets and the people's joy, solemnly placed the ark of the covenant in the place prepared for it. How then can I, the most miserable and the poorest of human creatures, who can hardly spend one-half hour in uninterrupted devotion, bring you within my house? I wish indeed that I could even once spend a half-hour in a worthy and proper manner!

Lord God, how devotedly did those three men strive to please you! And alas, how little do I do! How little time I give to preparing myself to receive Holy Communion!

Seldom am I able to concentrate my thoughts; seldom indeed is my mind free from distractions. Yet surely no foreign thoughts should enter my mind when I am in the life-giving presence of your Godhead. Nor should my heart be filled with any longing for any creature—for it is not merely an angel, but the Lord of the angels, whom I am preparing to receive as my guest.

There is a great difference between the ark of the covenant, with its "relics," and your most holy body, with its indescribable virtues; between those law-inspired sacrifices, which were figures of things to come, and the true Sacrifice of your body, which was the fulfillment of all the ancient sacrifices.

Why am I not more ardent and zealous in looking forward to your adorable presence? Why is it, indeed, that I do not prepare myself more conscientiously to receive *your* holy gifts, when those holy patriarchs and prophets of old—some of them kings and princes—led the whole people in showing a loving devotion to your divine service?

David, a most devout king, danced before the ark of God with all his skill, thinking of all the benefits that had been given in earlier times to his forebears. He fashioned various kinds of musical instruments, composed many psalms, and arranged for them to be chanted with fervor. He often played the harp, feeling the inspiration of the grace of the Holy Spirit. He taught the people of Israel to praise God with all their hearts, and to lift their voices in song to bless and praise him every day.

If such was the devotion and such the celebration in praise of God in the presence of the ark of the covenant, how much reverence and devotion ought I and all Christian people to maintain during the distribution of the Blessed Sacrament, when the most precious Body and Blood of Christ are received?

A great many persons take themselves to various shrines of departed saints. Such persons, full of admiration for the saints' deeds, look with awe at the spacious buildings on the grounds of the shrines and are inspired by everything connected with the memorials.

But you, my God, I can behold here present with me on your altar—you, who are Saint of saints, Creater of all humanity, and Lord of the angels.

It often happens that those on pilgrimage are motivated by curiosity, by the novelty of seeing new places, but bring little or no fruit of self-amendment back with them when they return home. That is especially true of those who move thoughtlessly from shrine to shrine, without any authentic contrition in their hearts. But here, my God, in the Sacrament of your altar, you are wholly present—the man Christ Jesus. Here is granted, to all worthy and devout communicants, the abundant fruit of eternal salvation. Neither levity nor curiosity nor sensuality draws persons here, but only a firm faith, a devout hope, and a sincere charity.

O God, unseen Creator of the world, how wonderfully you deal with us; how pleasantly and graciously you arrange everything that concerns your chosen ones, to whom you offer yourself to be received in this sacrament. Truly, this gift is beyond our understanding; it most powerfully attracts the hearts of those who are devout and strengthens their affection for you. Even your most faithful followers, whose whole life is devoted to self-amendment, grow in their devotion and their love for virtue through the mighty grace of the most Blessed Sacrament.

How amazing is the hidden grace of this sacrament, which only those who are faithful to Christ can experience! Unbelievers and those who have enslaved themselves to sin can have no experience of it. In this sacrament, grace is bestowed on, and lost virtue is restored in, the soul; and whatever of her beauty was disfigured by sin is restored. So powerful is this grace that, because of the devotion of those who receive it, both the soul and the weakened body feel the strengthening effects of its presence.

Even so, it is lamentable and pitiable that, in our lukewarmness and indifference, we are not drawn with a stronger desire to receive Christ, in whom lie all the hope and all the merit of those who will be saved. For he is both our sanctifier and our redeemer; he is our consoler during our pilgrimage on earth and the unending joy of the saints.

It is therefore most regrettable that so many persons give little thought to this saving Mystery, which is the source of joy in Heaven and supports the continued existence of the universe.

Alas, the blindness and hardness of the human heart not only keep many from having a tender affection for so great a Gift, but the daily reception of it likewise leads many to sink into a nonchalant carelessness about it! If this most holy sacrament were celebrated in only one place on earth and were consecrated only by the world's one priest, how strongly would people desire to be in that place, with that priest of God, so that they might witness the celebration of these divine mysteries! As it is, many are ordained priests, and Christ is offered in many places. So that the grace and love of God for human creatures might be more fully appreciated, this sacred Communion is made available widespread throughout the world.

Thanks be to you, O merciful Jesus, eternal Shepherd, for your desire to refresh us, in our state of poverty and banishment, with your own precious body and blood, and for your invitation to receive these mysteries, spoken from your own mouth: "Come to me, all you who labor and are heavily burdened, and I shall refresh you."

ii. *The Blessed Sacrament shows us the surpassing goodness of God and his love for us.*

THE DISCIPLE:

With confidence in your goodness and mercy, O Lord, I come near, like a sick person to the Physician, like a hungry and thirsty person to the Fountain of Life, like a wretched beggar to the King of Heaven, like a servant to his Lord, and like a forsaken soul to his kindly Comforter. But how is it that this should happen to me—that you should come to me? Who am I that you should make a gift of yourself to me? How can I, a sinner, dare to appear in your presence? And why would you decide to approach such a sinner?

You know your servant well, Lord, and are aware that I have in me nothing good of my own, nothing with which to win this favor you show me. Hence I can only admit my lowliness and acknowledge your goodness. I praise your tender mercy and thank you for your surpassing love. For I see that you come to me entirely on your own initiative, not for any merit of my own, simply so that your goodness will become better known to me, your love more readily shared with me, and your gracious humility more prominent to my sight.

Because it pleases you to do so, and because you have commanded that it be so, I willingly accept your courtesy as very pleasing to me and hope that my own sinfulness will not be an obstacle to it.

Sweetest and kindest Jesus, how thankful and reverent and full of praise we ought to be when we receive your sacred Body and Blood. Their precious value no human words can express!

At this communion, how shall I frame my thoughts when approaching you, my Lord, whom I cannot adequately honor but whom I have no choice but to desire to receive in a devout manner? What better or more profitable thought could I have than to humble myself entirely before you and proclaim your goodness—so infinitely far beyond my own. I praise you, O God, and shall proclaim you forever; I despise myself and cast myself down at your feet, sunk in the depths of my lowliness. You are the Holy of holies; I, the most sinful of sinners.

Yet behold, you turn your eyes upon me, who am unworthy even to look toward you. Behold, you come toward me; and because you desire to be with me, you invite me to your banquet! It is your wish that you give me the food of Heaven, the bread of angels, to eat— none other than your very self, the Living Bread which came down from Heaven and gives life to the world.

I am amazed to consider whence such love could proceed, and what a gracious consideration it is on your part to shine forth so. For such a gift, how great ought our thanks and praise to be! How useful and profitable was your guidance when you chose to offer it; and how sweet and satisfying this banquet, which you gave to be our food! How admirable are your ways, O Lord, how mighty your power, how unutterable your truth! For you did but speak the word and the universe was made; what you commanded, that is what was done.

It is a great marvel, worthy of faith but beyond human understanding, that you, Lord God, who are true God and true man, have offered yourself completely to us, in a little bread and wine, and in that form have become our never-failing support. You who are the Lord of the universe and are without any need for it, are nevertheless pleased to dwell in us by means of this sacrament.

Keep my heart and body unblemished by sin, so that

with a cheerful and upright conscience I shall often be able to celebrate and receive, to my everlasting benefit, these mysteries, which you yourself established and commanded to be celebrated in your honor, as an everlasting memorial.

Rejoice, my soul, and give thanks to God for so noble a gift, so precious a comfort, granted you in this vale of tears. Whenever you call to mind this mystery and receive the Body of Christ, you review the work of your redemption and are made a sharer in all the merits of Christ. The love of Christ never wanes, and the power of his atoning sacrifice is never exhausted. Teach yourself, therefore, to prepare for it by constantly renewing your heart and giving careful attention to this great mystery of salvation. As often as you celebrate or attend these holy mysteries, they should seem as wonderful, new, and joyful as on that day when Christ first descended into the womb of the Virgin, or when he hung on the cross and suffered and died for the salvation of mankind.

iii. *Frequent reception of Holy Communion is desirable and profitable.*

THE DISCIPLE:

Look upon me, O Lord, as I come to you, so that your gift may bring me blessing, and so that I may rejoice in your holy banquet, which you have prepared for the poor out of your goodness, O God. Behold, all that I can or should desire is found in you. You are my salvation and redemption, my hope and strength, my honor and glory. May the soul of this, your servant, therefore rejoice in you, for unto you, O Lord, I have lifted up my soul. I long to receive you at this occasion with devotion and reverence. I desire to welcome you into my house so that, like Zacchaeus, I might be considered worthy to have your blessing and be numbered among the children of Abraham.

My soul longs to receive your Body and Blood; my heart longs for union with you.

If you give yourself to me, it is enough; for apart from you, there is no comfort. Without you, I have no life; unless you visit me, I have not the strength to live. So I feel strongly impelled to draw near you and receive you as the medicine of my soul; otherwise, I may faint along the way if I am deprived of the food of Heaven. It is just as you, most merciful Jesus, once said after preaching to the people and curing many of their illnesses: "I shall not send them home hungry, lest they faint on the way" (Matthew 15.32; Mark 8.8). May you deal with me in the same manner, for you chose to make yourself available as a comforter of your followers through this sacrament. You are the soul's sweet sustenance. And the person who worthily is nourished by you will inherit a share in your everlasting glory.

I, who so often fall into error and sin and who so quickly tire and faint, find the Blessed Sacrament to be a necessity. By means of frequent prayer, confession, and reception of your holy Body and Blood, I renew and cleanse myself, and stir up my devotion, fearing that if I abstain for too long, it might happen that I grow lax in my spiritual resolves.

A person's inclinations "are prone toward evil from

his youth" (Genesis 8.21). And unless there be some divine assistance for him, he will in time lapse into worse things. But Holy Communion draws us back from what is evil and strengthens us in what is good. If I am often inattentive or lukewarm when I celebrate or receive this sacrament, what would my spiritual condition be like if I did not receive this remedy and did not even seek after so powerful a help?

And though I am neither fit nor properly disposed to celebrate it every day, I will nevertheless try to receive the divine mysteries at proper times and be a sharer in its graces. For this is the greatest consolation of faithful souls for as long as they are absent from you, Lord, in their mortal bodies: that they often receive their Beloved with a devout intention, ever mindful of their God.

It is a wonderful sign of your graciousness and tender mercy toward us, O God, that you, who are the Creator and Giver-of-life to all spirits, should stoop to visit a lowly soul, abundantly satisfying its famishing hunger with your own divinity and humanity. How happy those minds and blessed those souls who have this privilege of receiving you, their Lord and God, with perfect affection. Those who receive you so are full of spiritual joy. And how great a Lord they entertain! How beloved is the Guest whom they honor! How delightful a companion do they welcome! How lovely and noble a spouse do they embrace!—the One who is to be loved before all others who are beloved, and desired above all else that can be desired. May you, most sweet and beloved Lord, let Heaven and earth and all their treasures keep silence in your presence. For all their glory and beauty have their origin in your own gracious bounty. They will never equal your name in grace or glory: your wisdom cannot be measured or told.

iv. *Those who devoutly receive Holy Communion merit many spiritual benefits.*

THE DISCIPLE:

My Lord and God, guide your servant with your sweet blessings so that I may approach your wondrous sacrament with devotion and worthiness. Lift my heart up to you and free me from my heavy weariness. Visit me with the grace of salvation so that my soul may taste your sweetness, lying hidden within this sacrament like water within a fountain. Give my eyes the power to see so deep a mystery, and strengthen my faith to believe it without reservation. For this mystery is your work, not something brought about by human power; it is your sacred institution, not a human invention.

No human being could comprehend or understand such things, which are beyond even the keener minds of the angels. So how could I, an unworthy and sinful person, a thing of dust and ashes, expect to penetrate and understand so high and so sacred a mystery?

O Lord, it is in simplicity of heart, in firmness and soundness of faith, and in obedience to your command that I draw near you, with hope and reverence. And I do sincerely believe that you are present here in this sacrament, both God and man.

It is your desire that I should receive you and unite

myself with you in charity. I therefore beg for your mercy and ask you for one special grace, namely, that I may be entirely "dissolved" within you and overflow with love for you, and thus receive thereafter no consolation but what comes from you.

In this highest and most precious sacrament are the health of both soul and body, the medicine for all my spiritual dullness, the cure for all my vices, and the bridle for all my appetites. It overcomes or at least weakens my temptations, infuses new grace, increases my virtue, confirms my faith, strengthens my hope, and stirs up and enlivens my charity.

O God, you who are the protector of my soul, the repairer of human weakness, and the source of all spiritual consolation, you have bestowed—and often still bestow—many blessings through this sacrament on your beloved ones who receive Communion devoutly. You comfort them in the face of every manner of trial and lift them up from their deep dejection so that they can hope in your protection; and you renew and enlighten them spiritually, with new grace. Hence those who, before receiving Communion, are at first full of anxiety or lacking in magnanimity, find themselves afterward refreshed and changed for the better by the heavenly food and drink.

You have chosen this manner of dealing with your faithful ones so that they might experience and acknowledge their own weakness and the benefits and grace they have received from you. For they, in themselves, are cold, hard-hearted, and lacking in devotion; but you enable them to become fervent, cheerful, and devout. When, indeed, has anyone ever approached the fountain of your sweetness in humility without returning with at least some of your own sweetness? Or who could stand near a large fire without receiving some of its heat? You are the ever-full and overflowing fountain, the ever-burning and unfailing fire.

Even though I am not able to draw water from the fountain itself or drink my full from it, I shall nevertheless put my lips to this heavenly stream, whence I can receive at least a small drop to refresh my thirst and keep from withering away.

So too, though I cannot as yet be altogether heavenly or as fervent as the cherubim and seraphim, I shall apply myself devoutly and earnestly to prepare my heart to experience even a small flame of the divine fire by receiving the Blessed Sacrament with a humble disposition.

In this effort, my most merciful and holy Savior Jesus, may you in your gracious bounty supply whatever is wanting in me. For you have graciously chosen to call us all unto yourself, saying, "Come to me all you who labor and are heavily burdened, and I shall refresh you." I labor, indeed, "by the sweat of my brows" (Genesis 3.19). I am tormented by a grieving heart, troubled by temptations, confused and weighted down by evil tendencies—and there is no one except you, my Lord, God, and Savior, to whom I can entrust myself and everything I can call mine, so that you may keep watch over me and bring me safely to life everlasting.

May you welcome me for the honor and glory of your name, because you have prepared your body and blood to be my food and drink.

O Lord God, my Savior, grant that the zeal of my devotion may increase through my frequent reception of your Mysteries.

v. *The dignity of the priesthood is a sharing in the dignity of the Blessed Sacrament.*

THE VOICE OF CHRIST:

If you were as pure as the angels or as holy as Saint John the Baptist, you would not be worthy to receive this sacrament yourself or administer it to others. For it is not within what human beings can call their due that any man should consecrate and administer the Sacrament of Christ or receive as food the Bread of Angels.

Great is this mystery. Great also is the dignity of priests, to whom has been granted what is not allowed to angels. Only priests validly ordained in the Church have the power to officiate this sacrament and consecrate the Body of Christ. Indeed, the priest is but the minister of God, using the word of God by God's command and appointment. God is the principal author and the invisible worker, all things being subject to his will, all things obedient to his command.

Concerning this sacrament, you who are priests should place your faith, therefore, in God almighty rather than in your own senses or any visible evidence. And you must therefore approach this holy work with fear and reverence. Be circumspect and consider whose ministry has been conferred on you by the laying on of the bishop's hand. Take note that you have been made a priest and consecrated in order to celebrate the Lord's sacraments; and take care that you offer the Sacrifice to God in a faithful and devout manner, at proper times, and conduct yourself blamelessly. You do not carry a lighter burden now, but are bound by a stronger cord of discipline and are obliged to a higher degree of sanctity.

Every priest should be adorned with all the virtues and should give others an example of virtuous life. Neither his behavior nor his conversation should resemble the popular and usual ways of other people; rather, they should resemble those befitting the angels in Heaven, or perfect souls on earth.

A priest vested in sacred garments is Christ's deputy, and as such is to beseech God for himself and for the whole people, in all humility and with earnest intercession. The sign of the Lord's cross is before him and behind him, so that he may be constantly reminded of the passion of Christ. The cross he wears on the front of his chasuble so that he might look upon Christ's footsteps and seek to follow them. He has the sign of the cross also on the back of his chasuble so that he may cheerfully endure, for God's sake, any evils that others may inflict on him. He bears the cross before him so that he may mourn his own sins, and the cross behind him so that he may also have sympathy and compassion for the faults of others, aware that he is an intermediary between God and the sinner.

Nor should a priest grow weary of praying or of the Holy Offering till the grace and mercy he seeks have been obtained. For when a priest celebrates the Holy Eucharist, he causes the angels to rejoice and brings spiritual benefits to the Church; he assists the living, bestows rest on the departed, and wins for himself a share in all that is good.

vi. *Ask Christ to help you prepare for Holy Communion.*

THE DISCIPLE:

O Lord, when I compare your worthiness with my lowliness, I tremble uncontrollably and become confused and overwhelmed by fear. If I do not come to you, I shy away from Life; yet if I intrude unworthily, I merit your displeasure. What then should I do, O my God, my helper and advisor in every crisis? Teach me the right way; show me some brief devotion suitable for preparing myself to receive Holy Communion. For it is good that I know how to prepare my heart for you with devotion and reverence, either to receive your Blessed Sacrament for the health of my soul, or to officiate at so great and divine a Sacrifice.

vii. *Before receiving Communion, examine your conscience and resolve to amend your faults.*

THE VOICE OF CHRIST:

Above all, God's priest ought to prepare to celebrate, and to receive, the Blessed Sacrament with a surpassing humility of heart, with the reverence of a suppliant, with a mature faith, and with a conscientious desire to give honor to God.

Examine your conscience carefully, and purify and clarify it as much as possible through a sincere contrition and humble confession. Then there will be in you nothing to weigh heavily on you or stir you to remorse of conscience or hinder your freely approaching the throne of Grace. Look with displeasure on all your past sins, especially on those you tend to commit daily. And as time allows, confess to God all the miseries your unruled appetites have caused.

Make it your sad and painful lament that you are still worldly and flesh-centered, that your passions are still unmortified, and that the impulses of concupiscence are so abundant in you;

—that you are heedless about your outer senses and often caught up by foolish desires;

—that you are bent toward outer, material things, and negligent of inner, spiritual things;

—that you are given to excessive laughter and mirth, being slow and disinclined to tears and sorrow for your sins;

—that you are eager to be comfortable and to enjoy bodily pleasures, but indifferent to zeal and self-discipline;

—that you are curious to hear the latest news and to look at what pleases the eye, and loathe to welcome whatever is humble and socially repellent;

—that you are greedy to have an abundance, close-fisted in your generosity, and miserly in holding your goods;

—that you are so thoughtless in your speech, so unwilling to keep silent;

—that you are so boorish in your manners, so annoying in your conduct;

—that you are so food-centered, but so deaf to the word of God;

—that you look forward to your rest, but are slow to take up your work;

—that you can stay awake well enough to hear gossips' tales, but come drowsy to sacred vigils;

—that you long for the end of every devotion, being meanwhile an inattentive daydreamer;

—that you are so negligent about your prayers, so lukewarm in celebrating Mass, so dry and indifferent in receiving the Holy Eucharist;

—that you are so easily distracted, so seldom fully attentive;

—that your anger is so quick to flare up, while you look for opportunities to find fault with another;

—that you are quick to judge others, and severe in chastising them;

—that you are joyful enough in good times but downcast at the first sign of trouble;

—and that while you are always making good resolutions, you seem unable to bring them to any fruitful self-improvement.

When you have confessed and asked forgiveness for these faults, as well as any others, and learned to find your own weakness displeasing to yourself, firmly resolve to make an unrelenting effort to correct your behavior and make progress along the path to holiness. Then, make it your whole effort and desire to offer up your very self on the altar of your heart, as a living, continuous offering of your body and your soul, dedicating them in faith to me, in honor of my name.

If you do that, you may be considered worthy to approach unto God, to celebrate the eucharistic Sacrifice, and to receive the sacrament of my Body and Blood for the health of your soul.

For no one can have a more worthy offering, nor do anything more effective in washing away sin, than to offer himself entirely and unreservedly to God in and through the Holy Communion of Christ's Body and Blood.

And if a person does what he can and is truly repentant, no matter how often he may come to me for pardon and grace—"as I live, says the Lord God, I do not desire the death of the sinner, but rather than he be converted and live" (Ezekiel 33.11)—no longer shall I remember his sins; they will all be forgiven him.

viii. *Offer yourself along with the Body and Blood of Christ as a pure sacrifice to God.*

THE VOICE OF CHRIST:

When I did willingly offer myself up to God the Father in redemption of your sins, my hands were stretched out on the cross and my body was stripped and laid bare—and thus nothing remained with me that was not wholly offered in sacrifice to appease the divine anger. So too should you willingly offer yourself to me, daily, in Holy Communion, as a pure and sweet offering, with all your talents and affections, even to the very depths of your being.

What else have I ever asked of you than that you resign yourself entirely to me? Whatever you offer me *other than yourself* has no value in my sight; for it is *you* I seek, not your gifts.

And just as you would not be satisfied if you possessed everything except me, so you cannot please me, no matter what gifts you offer me, if you do not offer me yourself. If you offer yourself to me and give yourself up wholly to God, then your offering will be acceptable.

Recall that I offered myself wholly up to my Father on your behalf; and that I also gave my entire body and blood to be your food so that I might be wholly yours and you might remain mine till the end. But if you place your trust in yourself and decline to place yourself freely under the governance of my will, your offering is obviously halfhearted and there can be no complete union between us.

Before all else, therefore, make it your priority to place yourself in God's hands if you would obtain both liberty and grace. The reason why so few persons become spiritually free and enlightened is precisely this: they cannot bring themselves to renounce their selfishness entirely.

What I said once remains still true: "Unless a man forsake everything, he cannot be my disciple" (Luke 14.33). If it is your desire to be my disciple, therefore, offer yourself to me with your whole heart.

ix. *Offer up yourself and everything that is yours to God,
asking him for whatever you need.*

THE DISCIPLE:

"All things in Heaven and on earth are yours, O Lord"
(Psalm 24.1). I desire to give myself to you as a free offering and to remain yours forever after. This day, O
Lord, I offer myself to you, with a sincere heart and
humble submission, as an unending sacrifice in your
praise. Receive me, along with the holy offering of
your precious Body that I make to you today, attended
by the presence of unseen angels. May it bring me and
all your people to salvation.

Lord, I offer to you, on your own altar of reconciliation, all my sins and faults committed since that day
when I was first capable of sinning, even to the present
hour. I ask that you consume and burn them, one and
all, in the fire of your love. Wipe away the stain of my
sins. Cleanse my conscience from all errors. Restore to
me the grace I have lost by sin. Give me your complete
forgiveness, and in your mercy admit me to the kiss of
peace.

What else can I do concerning my sins but confess
and regret them in all humility, constantly asking for
your reconciliation. I ask that you be willing to restore
our friendship when I stand penitent before you, my
God.

I loathe my sins and am resolved never to commit
them again. But I also grieve over them, and will do
so as long as I shall live; for I am resolved to do penance
and, as much as I am able, make restitution for the
harm they have done.

For your name's sake, O God, forgive me my sins. Bring my soul to salvation, for you redeemed it with your precious body and blood. See how I place myself at your mercy and resign myself into your hands. Deal with me according to your goodness rather than according to my wickedness and iniquity.

I offer you all that is good in me, small and imperfect though it may be, and ask that you improve and bless it, making it worthy and acceptable to you, bringing it to ever greater perfection. And bring me—though I am only a poor, lazy, and useless servant—to a good and blessed end.

I offer to you also all the holy intentions of your devout servants—the needs of parents, friends, brothers and sisters, all who are dear to me, all who have done any good for me or for others because they love you. I commend to you also all those who have asked or begged that I pray or offer the divine Sacrifice for them and for those whom they love.

I pray that they may all feel the immediate help of your grace, the comfort of your consolations, protection from dangers, and deliverance from pain; and having been rescued from all evils, may they joyfully offer many prayers of thanksgiving to you.

I offer to you also my prayers and the redeeming power of your Sacrifice particularly for those who have in any way hurt me, caused me sadness, found fault with me, or brought me any harm or displeasure. I pray also for those whom I have at some time annoyed, troubled, burdened, or scandalized, by my words or my actions, knowingly or not, asking you to grant us all, equally, pardon for our sins and our offenses against each other.

Cleanse our hearts of all suspiciousness, wounded pride, anger, and contentiousness, anything that might conflict with charity or lessen our neighborly love.

Have mercy, O Lord, have mercy on all who ask you for mercy; give your grace to anyone in need of it; and remake us so that we may be worthy to enjoy your grace and go forward to eternal life. Amen.

x. *Do not keep yourself from receiving the Blessed Sacrament without good reason.*

THE VOICE OF CHRIST:

You should frequently approach the Fountain of grace and divine mercy, of goodness and holiness, so that you may be healed of your sins and passions and become more vigilant and stronger against the wiles and temptations of the devil. He, your enemy, knows well how much advantage (and restorative power) is received in Holy Communion, and he tries by every means and at every opportunity to distract faithful and devout persons and pull them away from partaking of it.

Hence it happens that some persons, when preparing themselves for Holy Communion, find themselves more beset by Satan's insinuations than they do at other times. That wicked spirit, as it is written in the Book of Job, goes among the children of God to trouble their minds with his accustomed malice, leading them to be overly scrupulous or uncertain in conscience, thus dampening their desire for the Sacrament. He may even make direct assaults on their faith. His purpose is either to try to persuade them to put off receiving Communion, or to receive it in a lukewarm manner.

But there is no need for anyone to fall prey to his subtle and false insinuations, no matter how hideous or filthy they may be. All such foolish imaginings are to be hurled back at his head! Simply despise and scorn the miserable wretch, and on no account decline to receive Holy Communion merely because of his assaults or the difficulties that may accompany them.

It often happens that persons become too anxious to attain a certain "degree" of holiness, or else worry about the effectiveness of previous confessions; they confuse and hinder themselves. You should instead follow the spiritual direction of the truly wise, and lay aside your anxiety and scrupulousness as hindrances of the grace of God and enemies of a devout soul. Do not let every small annoyance or trouble keep you from receiving Communion; rather, confess your sins at once and cheerfully forgive others any offenses they have committed against you. Likewise, if you have offended another, ask his pardon and God will also forgive you.

In what way are you better off by delaying the confession of your sins or the reception of Holy Communion? Make yourself thoroughly clean as soon as you can; spit out the poison with all speed; quickly apply this healing Remedy—and then you will find yourself better off than you would be if you delayed. If today you put off receiving the Sacrament for one reason, another stronger reason may well be yours tomorrow. Thus you may go on for a long time without receiving Communion, and gradually become less and less fit to receive it!

As quickly as possible, therefore, shake yourself from your present sluggishness and laziness; for you do yourself no favor to remain for a long time with a nagging conscience and full of anxiety, nor to isolate yourself from the divine Sacrifice because of day-after-day guiltiness.

Indeed, a lengthy abstention from Communion can do you serious harm, commonly leading you to a spiritual "drowsiness." Unfortunately, some lukewarm and unself-disciplined persons decide to put off confessing their sins, and the receiving of Communion too, because they are reluctant to keep stricter watch over their behavior!

How poor and middling are the devotion and charity of those who so lightly put off receiving Holy Communion!

On the other hand, how happy and how pleasing to God is that person who governs his life and keeps his conscience so pure that he is well prepared and disposed to receive the Blessed Sacrament even every day, if he has the opportunity and can do so without being conspicuous.

Yet if a person sometimes abstains from receiving the Sacrament out of humility or for a legitimate reason, his abstention is commendable if it is motivated by reverence. But if it is only a spiritual drowsiness that has fallen over him, he must shake himself awake and do whatever is in his power; and the Lord will assist his desire because of his good intention—which is what God counts most important. Even should such a person be hindered by some legitimate reason from receiving the Sacrament, but with a good will intends to receive it, he will not lose its fruits. For it is within the power of any devout person, every day at any hour, to draw near to Christ in a spiritual Communion, without any obstacle and with much profit. Whenever one devoutly calls to mind the passion of Christ and is filled with a fervent love for him, he receives a mystical Communion and is spiritually refreshed.

Still, on certain days and at the scheduled time, one ought to receive the Body and Blood of Christ the Redeemer sacramentally, with loving reverence, for the sake of the glory and honor of God, rather than fail to do so out of consideration for one's own convenience. The person who prepares himself only when a feast day draws near, or when compelled by local custom, will too often be *un*prepared.

Blessed are those who offer themselves as "burnt offerings" to the Lord whenever they either administer or receive Holy Communion.

Priests should be neither too slow nor too hurried in their manner of celebrating the Sacrament, but should follow the custom accepted among those with whom they live. They should also avoid a tedious manner, or

one that is disturbing to others, and follow the pre-
scribed ritual as established by their superiors. A
priest's manner of celebrating should serve the edifica-
tion of others present rather than reflect his own devotion or feelings.

xi. *The Blessed Sacrament and the Holy Scriptures are*
both needed by the faithful soul.

THE DISCIPLE:

O blessed Lord Jesus, how great is the happiness of the
devout soul who feasts with you at your Banquet—
where there is no food to be eaten besides yourself—
you the Most Beloved, you who are to be desired
beyond all other desires of the heart!

I too would find it a joyful thing to be in your presence and pour forth tears from the depths of my heart
and, like the grateful Magdalen, wash your feet with
my tears. But where now are those many holy tears, or
where is such devotion? Surely, in your sight and that
of your angels, my entire heart should be inflamed and
should weep for joy. For in this Blessed Sacrament I
have you truly present, though hidden under another
form.

My eyes could not bear to look upon you in your divine brightness; nor could the entire world survive if
exposed to the splendor of the glory of your majesty.
In this I see that you have considered my weakness and
have veiled yourself under this sacramental sign. In
this sacrament, he whom the angels adore in Heaven
I do truly possess and adore; yet I, for the present and

for some while to come, can do so only by faith, while they possess you directly by sight, not through a veil. For my part, I should be content with the light of true faith, and to walk in that light till the day of everlasting brightness dawns and the shadows of figures pass away. Then too, when that day of perfection comes, the use of sacraments will cease; for the blessed in Heaven, enjoying their heavenly glory, will have no need of any sacramental medicine. The blessed will rejoice forever in the presence of God, beholding his glory "face to face." And being transformed from their own brightness into the brightness of the unfathomable God, they "taste" the Word of God made flesh, as he was from the beginning and will ever remain.

When I consider these wondrous things, they become a source of heaviness and weariness to me, as does even all spiritual comfort: because as long as I do not behold my Lord directly, in his own glory, everything I can see or hear in this world seems to me as nothing by comparison.

O God, you are my witness that nothing can comfort me, no created thing can give me rest, but only you, my God, whom I long to see in life everlasting. So long as I remain in this mortal flesh, that is an impossibility. I must therefore teach myself much patience and place myself entirely at your service. O Lord, even your saints who now rejoice with you in the kingdom of Heaven, while they lived in this world had to wait in faith and patience for the coming of your glory. What they believed, I believe. What they hoped for, I hope for. Where your grace has carried them, I hope to come. Meanwhile, I shall walk in faith, strengthened by the example of your saints.

I also have your holy books as my comfort and as a guide for my life. More important, I have your most holy Body and Blood as a unique medicine and hospice.

In fact, I see that two things are both very necessary for me in this life; without them, this life of misery could not be borne. For while I live imprisoned in the flesh, I find that I have need of two things, namely, food and light. You have given me, in my weak and helpless state, your sacred Body for the refreshment of both my soul and my body; and you have placed your word as a lamp unto my feet. Without both of these gifts, I would be unable to live: for the word of God enlightens my soul, and the Blessed Sacrament is the Bread of Life. These two may also be called the two "tables," one placed on one side, the other on the other side, in the jewel-house of Holy Church. One table is that of the sacred altar, on which is the holy bread—the Body of Christ. The other table holds the holy doctrine, teaching the true faith to humanity, unceasingly leading us onward even beyond the veil, where the Holy of Holies dwells.

Thanks be to you, Lord Jesus, Light of everlasting Light, for the table of sacred doctrine, which you had prepared for us by your servants—the prophets, the Apostles, and other teachers.

And again thanks be to you, Creator and Redeemer of mankind, for you, as a sign of your love to the whole world, prepared a magnificent supper at which you set before us, not the traditional lamb, but your own most sacred Body and Blood. With this Sacred Banquet, you brought rejoicing to all the faithful, renewing them with the cup of salvation containing all the delights of paradise. The holy angels join us at this feast, but with a sweeter happiness.

How great and honorable is the office of God's priests! For to them is given the sacred words for the consecration of the Lord of Majesty in the Blessed Sacrament; which they bless with their own lips, hold with their own hands, receive in their own mouths, and administer to others.

How clean those hands ought to be; how unsullied the mouth; how holy the body; how unblemished the heart, where the Author of holiness so frequently enters! Nothing but what is edifying, no word but what is good to speak and profitable to hear, ought to escape the mouth of a priest, who receives the Sacrament of Christ so often.

Likewise, how honest and chaste ought to be the eyes of him who often looks upon the Body of Christ; how spotless the hands so often lifted up to Heaven, hands that touch the Creator of Heaven and earth. In the law of God, what is commanded applies especially to the priest: "Be holy, just as I, the Lord your God, am holy" (Leviticus 19.2, 20.26).

O almighty God, assist us with your grace, particularly those of us who have undertaken the office of your priesthood, so that we may serve you devoutly and well, in purity of life, and with an upright conscience. And if it should happen that we do not live the innocency that befits our vocation, grant us at least the grace to lament our sins, and then, with a humble spirit and a good will, to resolve to serve you more conscientiously in the days left to us.

xii. *Prepare yourself for reverent reception of Christ in Holy Communion.*

THE VOICE OF CHRIST:

I, who am the lover of purity and the bestower of sanctity, look for a pure heart wherein to find my place of rest. "Prepare for me a large, furnished upper room, and I shall keep the Passover at your house with my disciples" (Mark 14.14-15, Luke 22.11). If you wish me to come unto you, and remain with you, "cast out the old yeast" (1 Corinthians 5.7) and sweep clean the dwelling within your heart. Shut out the whole world and its throngs of sins; sit like a sparrow alone on the housetop, and consider well your own sins with sadness of soul.

Every lover will naturally prepare the best and fairest home for his beloved; and this is a sign of the affection he has for his beloved.

Yet it is also true that there is no way in which you can make an adequate preparation for me, no matter what you might do, even if you spent an entire year doing nothing but preparing yourself. It is only by my grace and favor that you have permission to approach my table. It is as if you were a beggar approaching a rich man's banquet, with no way to return his hospitality except to give him humble thanks.

Do what is within your power, and do it diligently— not because you have to, or because you are following the local custom. With piety, reverence, and affection, receive the Body and Blood of your beloved Lord God whenever he indicates his desire to come unto you.

It is I who have called on you, I who have commanded you to prepare for my coming, and I who will supply for what you lack: come, then, and receive me.

Whenever I bestow on you the grace of devotion, offer your thanks to God; you have received the grace because I took mercy on you, not because you were worthy of it. If you lack the grace of devotion and feel yourself spiritually dry, give yourself without delay to prayer, to sighing and knocking, never ceasing till you are granted some drop or crumb of saving grace.

It is you who need me, not I you. It is I who can sanctify and strengthen you, not the other way around. Come to me to be sanctified by me, and unite yourself with me so that you may receive additional grace and be inspired to renew your efforts to amend your life. Be careful that you do not neglect this grace; use it to prepare your heart conscientiously, and then receive your Beloved into your soul.

Of course, you should not be concerned only to *prepare* yourself for devout reception of Holy Communion. After you have received me, make an effort to prolong my presence. A careful watch over your behavior after receiving Communion is just as important as your devout preparation beforehand. Keeping up your guard afterward is the best way to prepare yourself for receiving an increase in grace. For if a person turns at once to worldly amusements, he makes himself little disposed to devoutness of life.

Beware especially of idle talk. After Communion, remain in some quiet place and enjoy your God; for you have within you One whom nothing in the world can take from you.

I am the One to whom you should dedicate yourself completely, so that you no longer live for yourself, but *in me,* and thus enjoy freedom from every mental anguish.

xiii. *A devout soul will strive for union with Christ in the Blessed Sacrament.*

THE DISCIPLE:

Lord, I ask only for this one favor: that I might find you alone, by yourself, and open up my heart to you, enjoying your presence as my soul most desires. I would have no one else pay attention to me or interest me or hold me in any affection—so that only you might speak to me, and I to you, as a lover would speak to the beloved, and as a friend would feast with a friend.

What I ask and long for is that I might be completely united with you, having first withdrawn my heart from material things; and also that, through the frequent celebration of the Holy Eucharist, I might cultivate my taste for heavenly and eternal things.

Lord, God, when shall I be fully united with you? When fully embraced by you? When completely forgetful of my self-interest? You have said, "Live in me, as I live in you" (John 15.4). Grant that I also may continue to live as one with you.

For truly you are my Beloved, chosen from among thousands; in you my soul is well pleased to live all the days of her life. Truly, you are my Peace-maker; in you I find perfect peace and rest, while apart from you are toil and sorrow and unending misery. Truly, you are the hidden God, and you have no dealings with the wicked; you speak only to the humble and simple-hearted.

How gracious is your Spirit, O Lord, for he refreshes your children with the sweetest Bread, which comes from Heaven, to show them your own sweetness. There is no nation so great or so close to its gods as your faithful ones are close to you, our God. To us, as a daily courtesy, you offer yourself to be eaten and enjoyed, so that our hearts might be lifted up to Heaven.

Where is the nation so famous as the Christian people? What creature under Heaven is more beloved than the devout soul into whom God himself enters, and whom he nourishes with his own glorious flesh?

O grace indescribable, hospitality most admirable! What love beyond measure has been bestowed upon the human race!

What return shall I make to the Lord for his grace, for his incomparable charity toward me? There is nothing within my power more acceptable to give him than my own heart, uniting it perfectly with him. Then will my innermost being rejoice, when my soul is completely united with God. Then will he say to me: "If you desire to be with me, I desire to be with you." And I shall reply: "May it be your will, O Lord, to remain with me, and I shall gladly be with you. For it is my one desire that my heart be united with you."

xiv. *Pray for a fervent desire to receive the Blessed Sacrament.*

THE DISCIPLE:

How overwhelming is the happiness, O Lord, that you have prepared for those who fear you! Lord, when I think of those devout persons whom I have seen approach your Blessed Sacrament with the utmost devotion and affection, I am often embarrassed and blush secretly, knowing that I come to your altar, to the table of Holy Communion, so lukewarm in disposition.

It grieves me to know that I remain so indifferent, with so little affection in my heart; to know that I am not fully inflamed in your presence, my God; to know that I am not strongly drawn and affected, the way many devout persons have been. They, with a strong desire for Communion and a stirring affection of heart, could hardly keep themselves from weeping. For with the "mouth" of the heart, as well as that of the body, from the innermost part of their being they longed to receive you. They appeared to have no other way to temper or satisfy their hunger than to receive your Body, O God, the Fountain of Life, with spiritual eagerness and delight.

Indeed, the burning faith of such persons amounts

to probable evidence for your sacred presence in the Eucharist! They whose hearts burn so fervently truly know their Lord in the breaking of the bread, while you, Lord Jesus, walk along with them and converse with them.

Alas, affection and devotion and strong, fervent love, such as theirs, are too often far from me. O Jesus, turn with favor and mercy toward me, and grant that I, a poor and needy creature, may at least sometimes experience something of your own hearty and affectionate love when I receive Holy Communion. Grant that my faith may be strong, that my hope in your goodness may increase, and that after I have tasted this heavenly Manna, my charity, once it is perfectly aflame, may never die.

Yet I know that, in your mercy, you can grant me the grace I long for, on any day you please to do so, most kindly visiting me with fervor of soul. Even though I do not now burn with as strong a desire as that of those who are more perfectly devoted to you, it is with the help of your grace that I have this present desire for a great increase in my longing to receive you. I pray and desire to be numbered among your more fervent lovers and joined with such a holy company.

xv. *Humility and self-denial are the surest ways to obtain the grace of religious devotion.*

THE VOICE OF CHRIST:

Make it your special desire to seek the grace of devoutness; ask for it fervently and wait for it with both patience and confidence. Receive it with gratitude, cherish it in all humility, and accept it for as long as God desires you to have it—until the day comes when he himself is pleased to come to you.

Whenever you feel little or no devoutness in your heart, let that be a source of humility; on the other hand, do not fall into a state of melancholy or give in to self-pity. It often happens that God bestows in one brief moment what he has for some time denied you. Sometimes too, when he does not grant your petition when you first ask, he grants it later on.

If it were the case that grace were ours for the asking and were given immediately, our weak nature could not handle it. The grace of devotion is something to be waited for, with a firm hope and an unpresumptuous patience. If for a time the grace seems to be withheld from you, or taken away from you, do not immediately conclude that the reason is some defect in yourself, such as your sins. It may happen that there is in you some small obstacle that prevents us from having it— though perhaps "small" is the wrong word for anything that could keep you from having so wonderful a blessing!

But if you can remove or overcome that obstacle, whether it be major or minor, you will obtain what you desire.

At the moment you give yourself wholeheartedly to God, and abandon your attempts to have this or that toy for yourself, simply placing all your trust in him, you will find yourself entirely at peace. Nothing could be more pleasing to our taste, nothing more delightful to us, than to accept the good pleasure of what God wills for us.

Hence whoever lifts up his heart entirely to God and keeps himself free from any excessive liking or disliking for any created thing—he is most deserving to receive graces, especially the gift of unfailing devotion. The Lord prefers to grant his blessings wherever he finds his vessels empty.

So the more fully a person gives up his attachments to material things, the more successful he is at holding himself in a kind of contempt and letting his selfishness die. Then, the more quickly will grace come to him; the more there will be of it too; and the higher it will lift up his "freed" heart. Then will he "see" and rejoice, then will his heart expand, because the Lord's hand is on him. Indeed, such a person will have put himself *in* the Lord's hand, for ever and ever.

Take note, therefore, that those persons who seek God with all their heart are rightly to be called blessed, for they have not received their souls in vain. They, in receiving the Blessed Sacrament, are graced with the even higher grace of divine union. Why? Because they have acted not so as to further their own devotion and happiness, but, beyond all such considerations, so as to give honor and glory to God.

xvi. *Lay your needs at the feet of Christ and ask for his grace.*

THE DISCIPLE:

O most sweet, most loving Lord, I desire to receive you with all devoutness. You know my weaknesses and the unavoidable hardships I endure. You know what evil-doings and sinful habits I have become involved in, how they weigh me down, disturb my mind, tempt my will, and cause me to despise myself. To you I come for healing, asking for your forgiveness and strength. I call upon you, for you know all things (including my most private thoughts) and best know how to comfort and help me. You know what blessings I most need; you know how bankrupt I am in virtue.

Look upon me as I stand before you, a poor, naked wretch calling upon you for grace, begging your mercy. Feed the hungry one who calls upon you; burn away his worldliness with the fire of your love; and give light to my blindness with the brightness of your presence. Teach me to find all earthly things bitter, to handle all grievances and setbacks with patience, and to lose all interest in contemptible material things. Lift up my heart, to you in Heaven, and do not send me away, a wanderer over the face of the earth. May you alone seem sweet to me, now and forever. For who but you can be my food and my drink, my love and my joy, my sweetness and all that is good in me?

I pray that, by your presence within me, you would set me afire, burn my old self away, and transform me into yourself. For I wish to be one in spirit with you, through the grace of a spiritual union and the melting power of an ardent love.

Do not send me away hungry and thirsty. Deal with me in the merciful way you have often dealt so marvelously with your saints. A marvel indeed it would be if I were to be wholly set on fire by you, and my self were to decay into nothingness! For you are an always-burning, never-fading fire; you are a heart-purifying love, which gives light to my understanding.

xvii. *Develop in yourself a strong desire and a burning love to receive Christ in the Blessed Sacrament.*

THE DISCIPLE:

I do long to receive you, O Lord, with a deep devotion and a burning love, with all the affection and fervor of my heart, just as many of your saints and other devout persons have longed for you. They, when they shared in your Holy Communion, were most pleasing to you because of the holiness of their lives and the fervor of their devotion. So it is also that I desire to receive you, my God, my everlasting Love, my total Good and limitless Happiness—with as much affection and in such appropriate awe and reverence as any of your saints ever had, or could feel, toward you. And even though my feelings of devotion do not rise up to that measure, I can still offer you the affection of my whole heart, as if I were the only person to have such thankful and ardent longings for union with you.

So also, whatever a conscientious mind can conceive or desire, I offer it to you with deep reverence and spiritual affection. I have no desire to hold anything back for myself; rather, I gladly and freely offer up to you myself and all that is mine to give.

O Lord my God, my Creator and Redeemer, I desire to receive you today with the same affection, reverence, praise, honor, gratitude, worthiness, and love as was shown by your own most holy mother, the glorious Virgin Mary. When replying to the angel who brought her the glad tidings of the Incarnation, she said in all humility and devotion: "Behold the handmaid of the Lord. Be it done unto me according to your word" (Luke 1.38).

And just as your blessed forerunner, the exemplary Saint John the Baptizer, while still enclosed in his mother's womb, was moved by the Holy Spirit to rejoice in your presence and leaped for joy; and just as years later, upon seeing you, Lord Jesus, walking with your disciples, he minimized his own importance and said with due respect: "The bridegroom's friend, standing nearby and hearing him, rejoices to hear the bridegroom's voice" (John 3.29)—in the same way, I wish to be roused with a holy and strong desire to offer myself up to you with my whole heart.

For the same reason, on behalf of myself and all those for whom I have an obligation to pray, I offer and present you with all the surpassing joys, the strong affections, the spiritual ecstasies, the supernatural enlightenings, and the heavenly visions experienced by devout souls, along with every virtue and every word of praise that has been or will be offered you by all the inhabitants of Heaven and earth: so that, for ever and ever, you may be praised and glorified as you deserve.

O Lord God, receive this wish and desire of mine: to give you praise without ceasing, blessing beyond measure, such as your own indescribable greatness merits and deserves. I offer my praises unto you, longing to do so every day at every moment. And with spiritual affection for them, I invite all the souls in Heaven and all the faithful servants on earth to join me in offering you this thanks and praise.

Let every people and every nation praise you in every language, and let them bless your most sweet and holy name with great joy and burning devotion. Let those who reverently and devoutly celebrate this incomparable Sacrament and receive it with a full faith be judged worthy to receive both grace and mercy from your hands. And may they pray to you with all humility on my behalf, for I am a sinner.

And when these same faithful ones have received the reward of their devotion, and are united joyfully with you, and rise comforted and wondrously refreshed from your Holy Table in Heaven, may they pause to hold me in remembrance.

xviii. *Approach the Blessed Sacrament as a humble follower of Christ, not as an analyst, and let your reason be taught by holy faith.*

THE VOICE OF CHRIST:

You know that you should avoid any pointless investigation of the Blessed Sacrament, especially out of mere intellectual curiosity, if you do not wish to find yourself in the deep waters of skepticism. The one who seeks to understand my majesty will be overpowered by its glory. God's powers are beyond human understanding. Of course, one may properly desire to seek to know what is true *provided* that one is willing to be taught and takes care to follow closely the sound teachings of the Fathers of the Church.

It is an admirable simplicity for a person to keep apart from disputes about difficult or petty matters and to continue along the well-marked, safe path of God's commandments. Many persons have lost the gift of devotion because of having tried to understand what was beyond their ability to understand. What is required of you is faith and a sincere life; not erudition, not the ability to plumb the depths of the mysteries of God. If you cannot understand even the lesser "mysteries" of the created world, how can you expect to understand those that are higher? Submit your mind to God, and your reason to faith, so that the light of true knowledge will be yours to the extent of your need and profit.

When some persons experience strong doubts about their faith or the Blessed Sacrament, do not fault them, for it is the work of the Enemy. Do not let yourself become anxious about your own faith; do not get involved in a dispute among your own thoughts or try to "answer" any doubts the devil may suggest to you. Rather, trust the words of God, and trust his saints and prophets. Then the wicked Enemy will flee from you.

It is often an advantage to a servant of God to experience such things. For the devil does not bother to tempt unbelievers and sinners, who are already his. It is the faithful and religious person whom he tempts and troubles in his several ways.

Be steadfast, therefore, in your simple and undoubting faith. And with the same reverence that a beggar would show, approach the Blessed Sacrament. If there is anything about it that your mind finds difficult to understand, place it firmly in the care of Almighty God. He will not deceive you. It is those persons who trust too much in themselves who are soonest deceived.

God walks with the simplehearted. He reveals himself to the humble and gives the gift of understanding to the little ones. He enlightens the minds of those whose minds are holy, while he hides his grace from those whose minds are proud or skeptical. The human intellect is weak and easily deceived; but true faith is never deceived.

That is why the use of reason and investigation into nature ought to begin with faith, rather than precede it or presume to evaluate it.

In the Blessed Sacrament especially, which is so holy and so excellent, faith and love both take the lead, and work in hidden ways in us. God, whose life is eternal and whose power is without limits and beyond our comprehension, has performed great and unsearchable things in Heaven and on earth. There is no way for us to trace out the details of his marvelous works. Indeed, if the works of God could be understood by our human reason, they could not rightly be called "marvelous" or "indescribable."